Theology of the Body for Beginners

THEOLOGY OF THE BODY
for beginners

�֍

A Basic Introduction to
Pope John Paul II's *Sexual Revolution*

Christopher West

ASCENSION
PRESS

West Chester, Pennsylvania

Nihil obstat: Rev. J. Brian Bransfield, STD
                       Censor Librorum
                       March 10, 2008

Imprimatur: +Justin Cardinal Rigali
                       Archbishop of Philadelphia
                       March 19, 2008

All Scripture quotations contained herein are taken from the Revised Standard Version of the Bible, copyright 1946, 1952, and 1971 by the Division of Christian Education of the National Council of Churches of Christ in the USA. Used by permission.

Published by Ascension Press
Post Office Box 1990
West Chester, PA 19380
Orders: 1-800-376-0520
www.AscensionPress.com

Cover design: Devin Schadt

Printed in the United States of America
10 11 12 13 9 8 7 6 5 4 3

ISBN 978-1-934217-85-6

CONTENTS

Abbreviations

CCC   *Catechism of the Catholic Church*, second edition (Libreria Editrice Vaticana, 1997)

DV   *Dominum et Vivificantem*, John Paul II's encyclical letter on the Holy Spirit (Pauline, 1986)

EV   *Evangelium Vitae*, John Paul II's encyclical letter on the Gospel of Life (Pauline, 1995)

FC   *Familiaris Consortio*, John Paul II's apostolic exhortation on the Christian Family (Pauline, 1981)

FR   *Fides et Ratio*, John Paul II's encyclical letter on Faith and Reason (Pauline, 1998)

GS   *Gaudium et Spes*, Vatican II's Pastoral Constitution on the Church in the Modern World (Pauline, 1965)

HV   *Humanae Vitae*, Pope Paul VI's encyclical letter concerning Human Life (Pauline, 1968)

LF   *Letter to Families*, John Paul II's letter in the Year of the Family (Pauline, 1994)

LG   *Lumen Gentium*, Vatican II's Dogmatic Constitution on the Church (Pauline, 1964)

LR   *Love and Responsibility*, Karol Wojtyla's (John Paul II's) philosophical work on sexuality (Ignatius Press, 1993)

MD   *Mulieris Dignitatem*, John Paul II's apostolic letter on the Dignity and Vocation of Women (Pauline, 1988)

NMI   *Novo Millennio Ineunte*, John Paul II's apostolic letter at the Close of the Jubilee Year (Pauline, 2001)

OL   *Orientale Lumen*, John Paul II's apostolic letter on the Light of the East (Pauline, 1995)

RM   *Redemptoris Missio*, John Paul II's encyclical letter on the Mission of the Redeemer (Pauline, 1990)

RH   *Redemptor Hominis*, John Paul II's encyclical letter on the Redeemer of Man (Pauline, 1979)

SE   *Springtime of Evangelization:* John Paul II's 1998 *ad limina* addresses to the Bishops of the United States (Basilica Press, 1999)

TOB   *Man and Woman He Created Them: A Theology of the Body*, John Paul II's general audience addresses on Human Love in the Divine Plan (Pauline, 2006)

VS   *Veritatis Splendor*, John Paul II's encyclical letter on the Splendor of Truth (Pauline, 1993)

WH   *Witness to Hope*, George Weigel's biography of Pope John Paul II (HarperCollins, 1999)

INTRODUCTION

In January of 2004, *Time* magazine opened a sixty-page spread on the issue of human sexuality with an article that, even though written from a secular perspective, asked some of the right questions:

> Of all the splendidly ridiculous, transcendently fulfilling things humans do, it is sex ... that most confounds understanding. What in the world are we doing? Why in the world are we so consumed by it? The impulse to procreate may lie at the heart of sex, but ... bursting from our sexual center is a whole spangle of other things—art, song, romance, obsession, rapture, sorrow, companionship, love, even violence and criminality—all playing an enormous role in everything from our physical health to our emotional health to our politics, our communities, our very life spans.
>
> Why should this be so? Did nature simply overload us in the mating department...? Or is there something smarter and subtler at work, some larger interplay among sexuality, life and what it means to be human? (*Time*, Jan 19, 2004, p. 64).

This "something smarter at work," that "larger interplay among sexuality, life, and what it means to be human" is precisely what John Paul II explored in great depth and with penetrating insight in his Theology of the Body.

The late Pope's Theology of the Body is creating quite a "buzz" in the Church today. In fact, it has already begun what many are calling a "sexual counter-revolution." It is spreading and it cannot be stopped. Still, for the vast majority of Christians, the content of John Paul's teaching remains an untapped treasure. Why? As papal biographer George Weigel observes, "The density of John Paul's material is one factor; a secondary literature capable of 'translating' John Paul's [Theology of the Body] into more accessible categories and vocabulary is badly needed" (WH, p. 343).

My book *Theology of the Body Explained* (revised edition, 2007) provides a thorough, 600-page commentary on John Paul II's revolutionary teaching on the body and sexual love. While this work manages to unfold the Pope's insights and make them more accessible, its sheer size and more academic style can still intimidate the average person. As I wrote in the preface to *Theology of the Body Explained*, smaller-scale efforts are also needed. In response to that need, I humbly present this short introduction.

The first edition of this book, which was released in 2004, was based on the English text of the Theology of the Body translated by the Vatican newspaper *L'Osservatore Romano*. This newly-revised edition is based on the much improved "critical edition" of the Theology of the Body, translated by Dr. Michael Waldstein and published by Pauline Books and Media (2006).

In addition to providing a more coherent and faithful translation of John Paul's teaching, Waldstein unearthed several undelivered addresses in the Theology of the Body series and translated them into English for the very first time. Waldstein also inserted the Pope's original headings and chapter divisions into the text, allowing us to understand John Paul's train of thought in new ways. All of this called for both a revised edition of both my commentary and my "beginners" book (which you now hold in your hands).

Those looking for a theologically sophisticated treatment of John Paul II's thought should turn to other resources and commentaries. My goal here, as the title indicates, is to simplify the Theology of the Body "for beginners." After laying an important foundation in chapter one, I outline in chapters two through eight the main ideas of the Pope's teaching according to the structure of his original manuscript. Chapter nine provides some concluding thoughts on the role of the Theology of the Body in the "new evangelization." I also include a glossary that not only offers definitions of key terms and phrases for quick reference, but also serves as a summary of the book itself. Finally, the resource section lists organizations that you can contact to learn more about the Theology of the Body.

As you proceed, keep in mind that popularizing John Paul II's Theology of the Body is virtually uncharted territory. Finding the best language, images, and anecdotes with which to do so is a difficult task and remains a work in progress. While my goal, of course, is to convey the essentials of the Pope's teaching, I cannot help but deliver it through my own filter. As does every interpreter of John Paul's work, I bring my own personal perspectives, gifts, and shortcomings to the table. As St. Paul says, "Test everything; hold fast to what is good" (1 Thessalonians 5:21).

I pray that this book helps open a new world for you. Indeed, if we take John Paul II's "sexual revolution" to heart, we will never see ourselves and the universe quite the same way again.

– Christopher West
May 2009

Chapter 1

WHAT IS THE THEOLOGY OF THE BODY?

*God "impressed his own form on the flesh ... in such a way
that even what was visible might bear the divine form."*
— CCC 704

"Theology of the body" is the working title Pope John
Paul II gave to the first major teaching project of his
pontificate. In 129 short talks delivered between September
of 1979 and November of 1984, the Pope offered the Church
and the world a rich, biblical reflection on the meaning of
human embodiment, particularly as it concerns sexuality
and erotic desire.[1]

Catholic theologian George Weigel describes John
Paul II's Theology of the Body as "one of the boldest
reconfigurations of Catholic theology in centuries"—"a
kind of *theological time-bomb* set to go off with dramatic
consequences ... perhaps in the twenty-first century." At this
point the Pope's vision of sexual love "has barely begun
to shape the Church's theology, preaching, and religious
education." But when it does, Weigel predicts, "it will
compel a dramatic development of thinking about virtually
every major theme in the Creed" (WH, pp. 336, 343, 853).

God, Sex, and the Meaning of Life

Why might the Pope's study of sexual love impact "every
major theme in the Creed"? Because sex is not just about

---

[1]   John Paul II drew the contents of these talks from a manuscript
entitled *Man and Woman He Created Them,* which he had complet-
ed just prior to his election as pope in October 1978. He actually
divided the manuscript into 135 talks but delivered only 129.

sex. The way we understand and express our sexuality points to our deepest-held convictions about who we are, who God is, the meaning of love, the ordering of society, and even the ordering of the universe. Hence, John Paul II's Theology of the Body is much more than a reflection on sex and married love. By reflecting deeply on the meaning of the human body and the biblical analogy of spousal love, John Paul II's catechesis illumines the entirety of God's plan for human life from origin to eschaton with a splendid supernatural light.

To ask questions about the meaning of the human body starts us on an exhilarating journey that—if we stay the course—leads us from the human body to the mystery of sexual difference; from the mystery of sexual difference to the mystery of a holy communion in "one flesh"; from the mystery of this union in "one flesh" to the mystery of Christ's Holy Communion with the Church (see Ephesians 5:31-32); and from the Holy Communion of Christ and the Church to the eternal Holy Communion of Father, Son, and Spirit. In short, pondering the deepest meaning of the human sexual-body leads us step by step into the heart of the mystery of God himself. In this way, John Paul II's Theology of the Body affords "the rediscovery of the meaning of the whole of existence ... the meaning of life" (TOB 46:6).

Christ teaches that the meaning of life is to love as he loves (see John 15:12). One of the Pope's main insights is that God inscribed this vocation to love as he loves *in our bodies* by creating us male and female and calling us to become "one flesh" (see Genesis 2:24). The resurrection of the body and the redemption in Christ have implications for the way we understand the body and the sexual relationship. Far from being a footnote in the Christian life, this new understanding "concerns the whole Bible" (TOB 69:8). The mystery of the redemption and the resurrection of the body plunges us into "the perspective of the whole gospel, of the whole teaching, even more, of the whole mission of Christ" (TOB 49:3).

Christ's mission is to restore the order of love in a world

seriously distorted by sin. And the union of the sexes, as always, lies at the basis of the human "order of love." Therefore, what we learn in the Pope's Theology of the Body is obviously "important with regard to marriage." However it "is equally essential and *valid for the [understanding] of man* in general: for the fundamental problem of understanding him and for the self-understanding of his being in the world" (TOB 102:5).

No wonder we are all so interested in sex! The union of the sexes is a "great mystery" that leads us into the heart of God's plan for the cosmos (see Ephesians 5:31-32). But, again, we must stay the course in our reflections on the body. This is easier said than done. A great many obstacles, prejudices, taboos, and fears can easily derail us as we face the enigma of our own embodiment as male and female. The temptation to "spiritualize" our humanity and, even more, to "spiritualize" Christ and the Church is constant and fierce. The enemy incessantly denies Christ come in the flesh (see 1 John 4:2-3). But only by pondering Christ's *body* can we understand our own.

Christianity Does Not Reject the Body

When it comes to religion, people are used to an emphasis on the spiritual realm. However, many people are unfamiliar, and sometimes even uncomfortable, with an emphasis on the body. But this is a false and extremely dangerous divide. Spirit certainly has priority over matter. Yet, the *Catechism of the Catholic Church* teaches, "As a being at once body and spirit, man expresses and perceives spiritual realities through physical signs and symbols" (CCC 1146). As bodily creatures, this is in a certain sense the only way we *can* experience the spiritual world—in and through the physical world, in and through our bodies. By taking on a body through the *Incarnation*, God humbly meets us right here—in our physical, human state.

Tragically, many Christians grow up thinking of their bodies (especially their sexuality) as inherent obstacles to the spiritual life. Many think Christian teaching considers their spirits to be "good" and their bodies to be "bad." Such thinking couldn't be further from an authentic Christian perspective! The idea that the human body is "bad" is actually a *heresy* (the obstinate denial of or obstinate doubt after the reception of baptism of some truth which is required to be believed by divine and Catholic faith) known as Manichaeism.

Mani (or Manichaeus), after whom this false teaching is named, condemned the body and all things sexual because he saw in the material world the source of evil. As Christians we believe everything God created is "very good" (see Genesis 1:31). John Paul II summarized the essential distinction as follows: If the Manichaean mentality places an "anti-value" on the body and sexuality, Christianity teaches that the body and sexuality "always remain a 'value not sufficiently appreciated'" (TOB 45:3). In other words, if Manichaeism says "the body is bad," Christianity says "the body is so good that you cannot even fathom it."

The problem with our sex-saturated culture, then, is not that it overvalues the body and sex. The problem is that it has failed to see just how valuable the body and sex really are. *Christianity does not reject the body!* In a virtual "ode to the flesh" the *Catechism* proclaims: "'The *flesh* is the hinge of salvation.' We believe in God who is creator of the *flesh*; we believe in the Word made *flesh* in order to redeem the *flesh*; we believe in the resurrection of the *flesh*, the fulfillment of both the creation and the redemption of the *flesh*" (CCC 1015, emphasis added).

The Sacramentality of the Body

The Catholic faith, if you have not already noticed, is a very fleshy, sensual religion. We intimately encounter God through the action of the Holy Spirit upon "signs drawn from" the material world: through bathing the body with water (baptism); anointing the body with oil (baptism, confirmation, holy orders, anointing of the sick); eating and drinking the Body and Blood of Christ (the Eucharist); the laying on of hands (holy orders, anointing of the sick);

confessing with our lips (penance); and the unbreakable joining of man and woman in "one flesh" (marriage).

How can we describe the "great mystery" of the sacraments? They are composed of matter and are God's chosen means by which, through the action of the Holy Spirit, we encounter God's spiritual treasures. In the sacraments, spirit and matter "kiss." Heaven and earth embrace in a union that will never end.

The human body itself is in some sense a "sacrament." This is a broader and more ancient use of the word than we may be used to. Rather than referring to the seven signs of grace that Christ instituted, when John Paul speaks of the body as a "sacrament," he means it is a sign that makes visible the invisible mystery of God. We cannot see God. God is pure Spirit. Yet Christianity is the religion of God's self-disclosure. God wants to reveal himself to us. He wants to make his invisible, spiritual mystery visible to us so that we can "see" him. How does he do so?

Most everyone has experienced that deep sense of awe and wonder in beholding a starlit night or a radiant sunset or a delicate flower. In these moments, we are in some way seeing the signs of the presence of God (more accurately, seeing his reflection). "The beauty of creation reflects the infinite beauty of the Creator" (CCC 341). And yet, what is the crown of creation? What more than anything else in God's creation "speaks" of divine beauty? The answer is man and woman and their call to fruitful communion. "God created man in his own image, in the image of God he created him; male and female he created them. And God blessed them and said to them, 'Be fruitful and multiply...'" (Genesis 1:27-28).

John Paul II's Thesis

This brings us to the thesis statement of John Paul II's Theology of the Body. "The body, in fact, and only the body," the Pope says, "is capable of making visible what is invisible: the spiritual and divine. It has been created to transfer into the visible reality of the world the mystery

hidden from eternity in God, and thus to be a sign of it"
(TOB 19:4). In other words, somehow the body enables
us to "see" spiritual realities, even the eternal mystery
"hidden" in God. How so?

Think of your own reality as a human being. Human
nature is both spiritual and physical. We aren't spirits
"trapped" in our bodies. The Church has always maintained
that we are embodied spirits, or spiritualized bodies.
Through the profound union of body and soul in each of us,
our bodies *reveal* or "make visible" the invisible reality of our
spirits. But the body does even more. Because we are made
in God's image, our bodies also make visible something of
God's invisible mystery. It is from this perspective that John
Paul wants to study the human body—not as a biological
organism, but as a *theology*, as a "study of God." The body is
not divine. But it is a "sign" of the divine mystery.

A sign is something that points us to a reality beyond
itself and, in some way, makes that transcendent reality
present to us. The divine mystery always remains infinitely
"beyond"; it cannot be reduced to its sign. Yet the sign is
indispensable in "making visible" the invisible mystery.
As the *Catechism* says, "Man needs signs and symbols to
communicate ... The same holds true for his relationship
with God" (CCC 1146).

We must carefully maintain the essential distinction
between spirit and matter and (even more) between
Creator and creature. Yet, at the same time, we must
affirm the profound relationship between these realities.
Christianity is the religion of God's union with humanity. It
is the religion of the Word (who is pure Spirit) made flesh!
In "the body of Jesus 'we see our God made visible and so
are caught up in love of the God we cannot see' " (CCC
477). God's mystery is revealed in human flesh—theology
of the body. This is not merely the title of a series of papal
talks; this is the very "logic" of Christianity.

If at first it appears odd to speak of the body as a
theology, it shouldn't upon further reflection. Think
about Christmas. We believe in the mystery of a God who
took on human flesh and was born of a woman. As John

Paul II says, "Through the fact that the Word of God became flesh, the body entered theology ... through the main door" (TOB 23:4).

The Divine Mystery

Several times already we have spoken of the "divine mystery" or the "mystery hidden in God from all eternity" (see Ephesians 3:9). What does this mean? In the Christian sense, "mystery" does not refer to some unsolvable puzzle. It refers to the innermost reality of God and to his eternal plan for humanity. These realities are so far beyond anything we can comprehend that all we can really utter is the word "mystery." And yet God is "knowable"—not based on our ability to decipher some divine puzzle—but because God has made himself known.

As the *Catechism* says, "God has revealed his innermost secret: God himself is an eternal exchange of love, Father, Son, and Holy Spirit, and he has destined us to share in that exchange" (CCC 221). This key statement summarizes the ultimate mystery of God and the meaning of human existence: love. God *is* love, as the apostle John tells us (see 1 John 4:8). Not only because he loves us, but because *within God* the three Persons of the Trinity live an "eternal exchange of love." This is "the central mystery of Christian faith and life. It is the mystery of God in himself. It is therefore the source of all the other mysteries of faith, the light that enlightens them" (CCC 234).

In John Paul's language, God is an eternal *Communion of Persons*. A "common union" (communion) of persons is established to the degree that two (or more) persons mutually "give" themselves to one another in love and service. No human explanation of the Trinity fully suffices to express the mystery of God. Nonetheless, we can discern from revelation that the Father eternally "begets" the Son by *giving himself* to and for the Son. In turn, the Son (the "beloved of the Father") eternally receives the love of the Father and eternally gives himself back to the Father. The love they share *is* the Holy Spirit who, as we say in the

Nicene Creed, "proceeds [eternally] from the Father and the Son."

And here is why we exist: Love, by its nature, desires to expand its own communion. God certainly didn't *need* anyone else. The love of the Trinity is perfect and complete in itself. Yet out of sheer goodness and generosity, God wanted to create a great multitude of other persons to share in his own eternal, ecstatic "exchange of love."

Icon of the Trinity, Image of Christ and the Church

So, once again, when we speak of the invisible "mystery hidden in God from time immemorial" we are speaking of the fact that (1) *God is a communion of love* and (2) We are *destined to share in that exchange.* This two-part "mystery" is what the human body signifies right from the moment of our creation. How so? Precisely through the beauty and mystery of sexual difference and our call to become "one flesh" (see Genesis 2:24).

God imprinted in our sexuality the call to participate in a "created version" of his eternal "exchange of love." In other words, God created us male and female so that we could image his love by becoming a sincere gift to each other. This sincere giving establishes a "communion of persons" not only between the sexes but also—in the normal course of events—with a "third" who proceeds from them both. In this way, sexual love becomes an icon or earthly image in some sense of the inner life of the Trinity. (I don't know about you, but I have never heard the media describe it that way.)

In addition to imaging the Trinity, sexual love is also meant to image the union of God with humanity. Christ's redeeming self-donation is a new outpouring of the Trinity's love on all of creation. The Church receives this love and attempts to reciprocate it. God endowed our bodies as male and female with the sacramental ability to convey this exchange between Christ and the Church. As St. Paul says, quoting from Genesis, "'For this reason a man shall leave his father and mother and be joined to his wife, and the two shall become one flesh.' This is a great mystery, and I mean in reference to Christ and the church" (Ephesians 5:31-32).

This passage from Ephesians 5 is a key text—perhaps *the* key text—for understanding the body and sexuality "theologically." Christ is the one who was sent by his Father in heaven. He also left the home of his mother on earth. Why? To give up his body for his Bride (the Church) so that we might become "one flesh" with him. Where do we unite sacramentally with Christ? In a most profound way in the Eucharist.

When all the confusions are cleared and the distortions are untwisted, the deepest meaning of human sexuality—of our creation as male and female and our call to communion—is "eucharist." John Paul II describes the Eucharist as *"the sacrament of the Bridegroom and of the Bride."* God created us male and female right from the beginning to live in a "holy communion" that foreshadows *the* Holy Communion of Christ and the Church. In turn, the gift of Christ's body to his Bride (celebrated in the Eucharist) sheds definitive light on the meaning of man and woman's communion.

I never met my father-in-law; he died before my wife and I met. But I admire him tremendously because of the following story. At Mass the day after his wedding, having just consummated his marriage the night before, he was in tears after receiving the Eucharist. When his new bride inquired he said, "For the first time in my life I understood the meaning of Christ's words, 'This is my body given for you.'"

The Spousal Analogy

Scripture uses many images to describe God's love for humanity. Each has its own valuable place. But both Old and New Testaments use the image of spousal love far more than any other. This is also the image favored by the greatest mystics of the Church.

The Bible begins in Genesis with the marriage of the first man and woman, and it ends in Revelation with another "marriage"—the marriage of Christ and the Church. Spousal theology looks to these nuptial "book ends" as a key for interpreting all that lies between. Through this lens we learn that God's eternal plan is to "marry" us (see Hosea 2:19)—to live with us in an eternal exchange of love and communion. Not only that but, pushing the analogy, through this union God wants to infuse our humanity with his divine life. Representing all of us, a woman who walked this planet once opened herself so profoundly to God's love that she literally conceived divine life in her womb. In this way, as the *Catechism* teaches, Mary perfectly fulfills the spousal character of the human vocation in relation to God (see CCC 505).

And here is what we learn from the Pope's Theology of the Body: God wanted this eternal "marital plan" to be so plain to us—so obvious to us—that he impressed an image of it in our very being by creating us male and female and calling us to become "one flesh."

The Nature of Analogies

At this point it is important to specify that we use spousal love only as an *analogy* of God's mystery. Analogies always indicate, at the same time, both similarity and substantial (in this case, very substantial) dissimilarity. Without this recognition, there is a danger of inferring too much about divine life, based on human life.

For example, God is *not* a sexual being. The mystery of love and generation in the Trinity is infinitely beyond that of human love and generation. Thus, the Eucharist as we have just described it is certainly not a "sexual encounter." This doesn't mean the analogy of sexual love is just wishful thinking or human projection. *God* is the one who inscribed an image of his own mystery in our humanity by creating us male and female. But this is just the point: We are made in God's image, not he in ours. The *Catechism* states this clearly: "In no way is God in man's image. He is neither man nor woman. God is pure spirit in which there is no place for the difference between the sexes. But the respective 'perfections' of man and woman reflect something of the infinite perfection of God" (CCC 370; see also CCC 42, 239).

If all analogies are inadequate, at the same time John Paul II believes the spousal analogy is the *least* inadequate. Speaking of the communion of man and woman and the life it begets, he states, "In this entire world there is not a more perfect, more complete image of God, Unity and Community. There is no other human reality which corresponds more, humanly speaking, to that divine mystery" (Homily, Dec. 30, 1981). As we press into this human reality as an image of the divine reality, we must simply be careful to respect the infinite difference between God and his creatures.

The Body and the Spiritual Battle

If God created the body and sexual union to proclaim his own eternal mystery of love, why do we not typically see them in this profound way? For example, when you hear the word "sex," what generally comes to mind? Is it the "great mystery" of the one-flesh union as a foreshadowing of Christ's union with the Church, or something, shall we say, a little less sacred?

Ponder this for a moment. If the body and sex are meant to proclaim our union with God, and if there is an enemy who wants to separate us from God, what do you think he is going to attack? If we want to know what is most sacred in this world, all we need do is look for what is most violently profaned.

The enemy is no dummy. He knows that the body and sex are meant to proclaim the divine mystery. And from his perspective, *this proclamation must be stifled.* Men and women *must be kept from recognizing the mystery of God in their bodies.* As we shall see more clearly later on, this is precisely the blindness that original sin introduced at the serpent's prompting. But have no fear: Christ came preaching the recovery of sight for the blind! (see Luke 4:18)

For now, the point to keep in mind is that the battle for man's soul is fought over the truth of his body. It is no coincidence that St. Paul follows his presentation of the "great mystery" of the "one flesh" union in Ephesians, chapter five, with the call to take up arms in the cosmic struggle between good and evil in Ephesians, chapter six. As the source of the family and life itself, the union of the sexes "is placed at the center of the great struggle between good and evil, between life and death, between love and all that is opposed to love" (LF 23). Therefore, if we are to win the spiritual battle, what St. Paul says we must do—I kid you not, look it up—is "gird [our] loins with the truth" (Ephesians 6:14). The Theology of the Body is John Paul II's clarion call for all men and women to do just that—to gird their loins with the truth that will set them free to love.

The Foundation of Ethics and Culture

The stakes are incredibly high in the cultural debate about the meaning of sex and marital love. As John Paul II observes, the communion of the sexes is "the deepest substratum [or foundation] of human ethics and culture" (TOB 45:3). What does this mean? In short, human sexuality has crucial meaning for, and an essential relation to, marriage and the family. And as marriage and the family go, so goes the culture.

This is why Karol Wojtyla (the future Pope John Paul II) wrote in his book *Love and Responsibility* that confusion about sexual morality "involves a danger perhaps greater than is generally realized: the danger of confusing the basic and fundamental human tendencies, the main paths of human existence. Such confusion must clearly affect the whole spiritual position of man" (LR, p. 66).

Think how intertwined sex is with the very reality of human existence. You simply would not exist without the sexual union of your parents—and their parents before them, and their parents before them, and their parents before them. Every human being is the end result of thousands upon thousands of indispensable sexual unions. Remove just one sexual union from your family tree, and you would not exist. Nor would anyone else who descended from that union. The world would be a different place.

When we tinker with God's plan for sex, we are tinkering with the cosmic stream of human existence. The human race—its existence, its balance—is literally determined by who is having sex with whom, and, in what manner. When sexual union is oriented towards love and life, it builds families and, in turn, cultures that live the truth of love and life. When it is oriented against love and life, the sexual act breeds death—what John Paul II grimly, yet accurately, describes as a "culture of death." A "culture of death" is a culture that, failing to recognize the infinite worth of every human person, *chooses* death as a "solution" to its problems.

Reclaiming the Truth About Sex

Is the connection between our sexual choices and the culture of death still unclear? Ask yourself: Why do we kill approximately 4,000 unborn babies every day in the United States alone? Because we are misusing and abusing God's great gift of sex. Make no mistake: in the final analysis, the abortion debate is not about when life begins. It is about the meaning of sex. What most men and women who fight for abortion want is not so much the "right" to kill their offspring, but the "right" to have unrestricted sex without consequences.

This is why John Paul II wrote in his landmark encyclical *Evangelium Vitae* (*The Gospel of Life*): "It is an illusion to think we can build a true culture of human life if we do not ... accept and experience sexuality and love and the whole of life according to their true meaning and their close inter-connection" (EV 97).

Such logic does not bode well for our culture. It is no exaggeration to say that the task of the twentieth century was to rid itself of the Christian sexual ethic. If we are to build a "culture of life," the task of the twenty-first century must be to reclaim it. But the often repressive approach of previous generations of Christians—usually silence or, at most, the incomplete "don't do it" mantra—is largely responsible for the cultural jettisoning of the Church's teaching on sex. We need a "new language" to break the silence and reverse the negativity. We need a fresh theology that explains how the Christian sexual ethic—far from being the prudish list of prohibitions it is often assumed to be—corresponds perfectly with the deepest yearnings of our hearts for love and union.

This is why John Paul II devoted the first major teaching project of his pontificate to developing the Theology of the Body. A return to God's original plan for the union of the sexes is the only adequate starting point for building a culture that respects the meaning and dignity of human life. But before we dive into the content of the Pope's teaching, we should look briefly at his basic method and approach.

The Pope's Method and Approach

In contrast to more conventional approaches that emphasize the objective categories of "being" and "existence," John Paul II's philosophical approach begins with human experience. He believes that if what the Church teaches is objectively true, then human experience—subjective as it is—should offer confirmation of that truth. Knowing that the Church's message "is in harmony with the most secret desires of the human heart" (CCC 2126), the Pope does not need to nor does he attempt to force assent to his proposals. Rather, he invites men and women to reflect honestly on their own experience of life to see if it confirms his proposals.

Those who have been turned off by judgmental moralizers will find this approach delightfully refreshing. The Pope imposes nothing and wags a finger at *no one.* He simply reflects lovingly on God's Word and on human experience in order to demonstrate the profound harmony between them. Then, with utmost respect for our freedom, he invites us to embrace our own dignity. It doesn't matter how often we have settled for something less. This is a message of sexual healing and redemption, not condemnation.

With this compassionate approach—the Gospel approach—John Paul shifts the discussion about sexual morality from *legalism* to *liberty.* The legalist asks, "How far can I go before I break the law?" Instead, the Pope asks,

"What is the truth about sex that *sets me free* to love?" and "Why did God make us male and female in the first place?" In short, what does it mean to be human as male and female? John Paul II turns to Jesus for answers, so Part I of the Theology of the Body is called "The Words of Christ."

In his responses regarding the body and sexuality, Christ actually points us to three different stages of the human drama. John Paul II looks at each in turn: 1) *Our origin* based on Jesus' discussion with the Pharisees about God's plan for marriage "in the beginning" (see Matthew 19:3-9); 2) *Our history* based on Jesus' words in the Sermon on the Mount regarding adultery committed "in the heart" (see Matthew 5:27-28); and 3) *Our destiny* based on Christ's discussion with the Sadducees regarding the resurrection of the body (see Matthew 22: 23-33). Only in light of where we have come from (our origin), where we are now (our history), and where we are headed (our destiny), can we understand both *what it means to be human* and *how we should live our lives.* These are the two fundamental questions the Theology of the Body seeks to answer.

Revelation teaches that there are essentially two ways of living the truth of our humanity in its totality: celibacy and virginity or marriage (see FC 11). So, continuing his analysis on the words of Christ, John Paul reflects on the meaning of Christian celibacy as a fully human—and, yes, fully "sexual"—vocation (if that seems like a contradiction, keep reading). Then, in Part II, "The Sacrament," the Pope reflects on marriage both as a *divine gift* and as a *human sign* of God's love. Only in light of these two dimensions of the sacrament are we capable of understanding the *why* behind the *what* of sexual morality.

Having set the stage in chapter one, the remaining chapters will introduce you to the main themes of each of the sections of the Pope's teaching (outlined on the following page).

Part I:

THE WORDS OF CHRIST

Chapter 2

BEFORE THE FIG LEAVES:
GOD'S ORIGINAL PLAN FOR THE BODY

"This is the body: a witness ... to Love."
– John Paul II (TOB 14:4)

If you have ever read anything John Paul II has written, you have certainly encountered one of his favorite passages from the Second Vatican Council: "Jesus Christ ... by the revelation of the mystery of the Father and his love fully reveals man to himself and makes his supreme calling clear" (GS 22). This is John Paul's anthem: Christ "fully reveals" what it means to be human. Thus, even though his goal in this cycle is to reflect on God's original plan for the sexes as found in the book of Genesis, the Pope begins with the words of Christ. Genesis, in fact, can only be fully understood in the light of Christ.

In the Beginning It Was Not So

When some Pharisees questioned Jesus about the meaning of marriage, they recalled to him that Moses allowed divorce. Jesus' reply provides one of the keys to understanding the Gospel: "For your hardness of heart Moses allowed you to divorce your wives, but from the beginning it was not so" (Matthew 19:8). In effect, Jesus is saying something like this: "Do you think all the tension, conflict, and heartache in the male-female relationship is normal? This is not normal. This is not the way God created it to be. Something has gone terribly wrong."

Here is an image I like to use to bring this home. It is as if we are all driving around town in cars with flat tires. The rubber is shredding off the rims; the rims are getting all dented up; and we just think this is normal. After all, everyone's tires look this way. According to the analogy, Jesus is saying to the Pharisees (and to all of us), "In the beginning, they had air in their tires."

So, if we want to know the meaning of the "one flesh" union, according to Christ, we have to go back to "the beginning," before sin distorted things. That is the standard. That is the norm. As we look at John Paul II's reflections on the creation texts, we will probably realize at a new level just how far we have all fallen from God's plan. But do not despair! Christ came into the world not to condemn those with flat tires. He came into the world to re-inflate our flat tires. We cannot actually return to the state of innocence—we have left that behind. But by following Christ we can receive God's original plan for the sexes and live it with Christ's help (see CCC 1615).

Original Human Experiences

John Paul takes a refreshing look at the creation stories. Rather than looking abstractly at God's original plan, the Pope wants to consider the first man and woman's *experiences* of the body and sexuality. We, of course, do not have any direct experience of the first man and woman's state of total innocence. Nonetheless, the Pope proposes that an "echo" of the beginning exists within each of us. The original human experiences, he says, "are always at the root of every human experience ... Indeed, they are so interwoven with the ordinary things of life that we generally do not realize their extraordinary character" (TOB 11:1).

We approach these experiences through "the symbolism of biblical language" (CCC 375). Symbolism is the most apt way to convey deep spiritual truths, which is what Genesis seeks to do. We need not get hung up on the modern assertion that science has "disproved" the creation stories in Genesis. The creation stories were never meant to be scientific accounts of the origin of the world. Scientific knowledge is certainly valuable as far is it goes, but it cannot tell us the spiritual *meaning* of our existence. For this, the divinely inspired authors of Scripture employed the symbolism with which we are familiar.

Here is an analogy. Consider the difference for a woman when her optometrist looks in her eyes and when her husband or boyfriend does so. The scientist is looking at her cornea and records the scientific facts. The lover is looking at her soul and proclaims something more poetic and inspired (we hope). Does the scientist "disprove" the lover? No. These are simply two perspectives on the same reality. The author of Genesis was not a scientist but a lover, inspired by God to proclaim the spiritual mysteries at the origin of the world and of mankind. We must keep this in mind as we examine the creation stories.

According to John Paul, three experiences in particular define the human person in the state of innocence: *solitude*, *unity*, and *nakedness*. Much ink can be spilt unpacking the Pope's profound reflections on these experiences (see my book *Theology of the Body Explained*). Here, of course, I am only presenting a basic sketch. As I do, see if you do not find an "echo" of these experiences in your own heart.

Original Solitude: The First Discovery of "Personhood"

"Then the Lord God said, 'It is not good that the man should be alone; I will make him a helper fit for him'" (Genesis 2:18). The most obvious meaning of this "solitude" is that the man is alone without woman. But the Pope mines a deeper meaning from this verse. This creation account doesn't even distinguish between male and female until after Adam's "deep sleep." Here Adam represents all of us— men and women (*adam* in Hebrew means "man" in the generic sense). Man is "alone" because he is the only bodily creature made in God's image and likeness. Man is "alone" in the visible world as a *person*.

When Adam names the animals, he also discovers his own "name," his own identity. He was looking for a "helper," but didn't find one among the animals (see Genesis 2:20). Adam *differs* from the animals. What does the human person have that the animals do not? In a word, freedom.

Adam is not determined by bodily instinct. He is created from "the dust" like the animals (he is bodily), but he also has the "breath of life" inspiring his body (see Genesis 2:7). An inspired body is not just *a* body but *some*body. A *person* can choose what to do with his or her body. Mere dust cannot.

In this freedom Adam experiences himself as a *self.* He is more than an "object" in the world; he is a "subject." He has an "inner world" or an "inner life." It is impossible to speak of the inner life of a squirrel or a chicken. It is precisely this "inner life" that the words "subject" and "person" capture. Despite some modern propaganda to the contrary, we know intuitively that chickens are not "people too." We owe special respect to all of God's creatures (see CCC 2415-2418), yet no other bodily creature shares the dignity of being created in God's image.

Why was Adam endowed with freedom? Because Adam was called to love, and without freedom, love is impossible. In his solitude, Adam realizes that love is his origin, his vocation, and his destiny. He realizes that, unlike the animals, he is invited to enter a "covenant of love" with God himself. It is this relationship of love with God that defines Adam's "solitude" more than anything else. Tasting this love, he also longs with all his being to share this love (covenant) with another person like himself. This is why it is "not good for the man to be alone."

In his solitude, therefore, Adam has already discovered his two-fold vocation: love of God and love of neighbor (see Mark 12:29-31). He has also discovered his capacity to negate this vocation. God *invites* Adam to love; he never forces him because *forced* love is not love at all. Adam can say "yes" to God's invitation, or he can say "no." And this fundamental choice is expressed and realized *in his body.* Solitude—the first discovery of personhood and freedom— is something spiritual, but it is "experienced" bodily. As John Paul says, the "body expresses the person" (TOB 7:2). We can also say, the body expresses the freedom of the person, or, at least it is meant to.

Reclaiming an abused phrase, God is entirely "pro-choice." He gave us freedom in the first place. But some choices negate our vocation to love. Some choices can *never* bring happiness. We *are* "free" in a sense to "do whatever we want with our bodies." However, we are not free to determine whether what we do with our bodies is good or evil. As Adam learned, this is a tree (the "tree of the knowledge of good and evil") from which he cannot eat, lest he die (see Genesis 2:16-17). Therefore, human freedom (i.e., "choice") is fully realized not by inventing good and evil, but by choosing properly between them.

All of these insights are "contained" in the experience of Adam's solitude. Freedom is given for love. It can lead to destruction and division, but it is intended to bestow life and establish unity. It is our *choice.*

Original Unity: The Communion of Persons

After Adam named all the animals without finding a lover among them, we can imagine his sentiment upon seeing the woman. Adam's cry, "This at last is bone of my bones and flesh of my flesh!" (Genesis 2:23) expresses absolute wonder and fascination.

Notice the bodily focus. Adam is fascinated with *her body* because, as the Pope points out, this "at last" is a body that expresses a person. All the animals he named were bodies, but not persons. We lose this in English, but for the Jews, "flesh" and "bones" signified the whole human being. Hence, woman's creation from one of Adam's bones (see Genesis 2:21-22) is a figurative way of expressing that both men and women share the same humanity. Both are persons made in God's image. Both are "alone" in the world in the sense that they are both *different* from the animals (original solitude); both are called to live in a covenant of love.

"Therefore a man leaves his father and his mother and cleaves to his wife, and they become one flesh" (Genesis 2:24). This experience of *unity* overcomes man's *solitude* in the sense of being alone without the "other." But it affirms everything about human solitude in the sense that man and woman are both persons different from the animals. The human union in "one flesh" is worlds apart from the copulation of animals. What is the big difference? Admittedly, it looks much the same biologically, but human sexual union is not merely a biological reality. It is also a spiritual and *theological* reality. The human body is meant to reveal and participate in the spiritual mystery of divine love. As the *Catechism* states, "In marriage, the physical intimacy of the spouses becomes a sign and pledge of spiritual communion" (CCC 2360). Animals are not capable of this "spiritual communion" because they are not spiritual. Their "dust" or matter is not "in-spired" (filled with the Spirit). They are not made in God's image.

Becoming "one flesh," therefore, refers not only to the joining of two bodies (as with animals) but is a "'sacramental' expression which corresponds to the communion of persons" (TOB 31:2). Recall our discussion on the "sacramentality" of the body. The human body makes visible the invisible mystery of God who himself is an eternal Communion of Persons; of God who himself is love.

Here the Pope presents a dramatic development of Catholic thinking. Traditionally, theologians have said we image God as individuals, through our rational soul. This is certainly true. But John Paul II takes it a step further when he states: "Man becomes the image of God not so much in the moment of solitude as in the moment of communion." In other words, man images God "not only through his own humanity, but also through the communion of persons which man and woman form right from the beginning." He even says that this "constitutes, perhaps, the deepest theological aspect of everything one can say about man." Finally, he observes that on "all this, right from the beginning, the blessing of fruitfulness descended" (TOB 9:3).

God could not have bestowed a greater purpose and dignity on sexual love. As was stated previously, marital union is meant to be an icon in some way of the inner life of the Trinity! If we could take in this one truth and reflect on it, we would never view sex the same way again. God, remember, is not sexual. The earthly image pales in comparison to the divine reality. Nonetheless, God created us as male and female and called us to communion as the primordial (original, fundamental) revelation of his own mystery in the created world. This is what the Pope means when he describes marriage as the "primordial sacrament" (see TOB 96). The whole reality of married life, of course, is a sacrament. But nowhere is the "great mystery" more evident than when the two become "one flesh."

Original Nakedness: Key to Understanding God's Original Plan

Having discussed the original experiences of *solitude* and *unity*, we are ready to explore the third original experience—*nakedness*.

After the words describing their unity, we read that "the man and his wife were both naked, and were not ashamed" (Genesis 2:25). Of all the passages in the creation stories, the Pope says that this one is "precisely the key" for understanding God's original plan for human life. That is a bold assertion. In short, if we do not understand the meaning of Genesis 2:25, we do not understand the meaning of our creation as male and female; we do not understand ourselves and the meaning of life.

But how can we understand original nakedness when we, having inherited the "fig leaves," have no direct experience of it? We do so only by contrast; by looking at our own experience of shame and "flipping it over."

A woman does not feel the need to cover her body when she is alone in the shower. But if a strange man burst into the bathroom she would. Why? The Pope proposes that "shame" in this sense is a form of self-defense against being treated as an object for sexual use. In the case of this woman, she knows that she is never, ever meant to be treated as a "thing" for someone's kicks. Experience teaches her that men (because of the lust that resulted from original sin) tend to objectify women's bodies. Therefore, the woman covers her body not because it is "bad" or "shameful." She covers herself to protect her own dignity from the stranger's "lustful look"—a look that fails to respect her God-given dignity as a person.

Take this experience of fear (shame) in the presence of another person, "flip it over" and we arrive at Adam and Eve's experience of nakedness *without* shame. Lust (self-seeking sexual desire) had not yet entered the human heart. Hence, our first parents experienced a total defenselessness in each other's presence because the other's look posed no threat whatsoever to their dignity. As John Paul poetically expresses, they "see and know each other ... with all the peace of the interior gaze" (TOB 13:1). This "interior gaze" indicates not only the sight of a body, but a body that reveals a personal and spiritual mystery. They saw God's plan of love (theology) inscribed in their naked bodies and *that is exactly what they desired*—to love as God loves in and through their bodies. And there is no fear (shame) in love. "Perfect love casts out fear" (1 John 4:18).

This is why "nakedness without shame" is the key for understanding God's plan for our lives—it reveals the original truth of love. Let this point sink in: God created sexual desire "in the beginning" to be the very power to love as he loves—in a free, sincere, and total gift of self. *This is how the couple described in Genesis experienced it.* Sexual desire was not felt as a compulsion or instinct for selfish gratification. The experience of lust comes only with the dawn of sin. Lust is a result of what we might call "flat-tire syndrome."

Since the first man and woman were "fully inflated" with God's love, they were entirely free to be a gift to one another. They were "*free with the very freedom of the gift*," as the Pope puts it (TOB 15:1). Only a person who is free from the compulsion of lust is capable of being a true "gift" to another. The "freedom of the gift," then, is the freedom to *bless*, which is the freedom from the compulsion to *grasp* and *possess*. It is this freedom that allowed the first couple to be "naked without shame."

As a result of sin, our experience of sex has become terribly distorted. In the midst of these distortions, we can tend to think that there must be something wrong with sex itself (the "body-bad/sex-dirty" mentality stems from this). But the distortions we know so well are *not* at the core of sex. At the core of sex we discover a sign of God's own goodness: "God saw everything that he had made, and behold, it was very good" (Genesis 1:31).

According to John Paul, nakedness without shame demonstrates that the first couple participated in this same vision of God. They *knew* their goodness. They *knew* God's glorious plan of love. They *saw* it inscribed in their bodies and they *experienced* it in their mutual desire. We lost this glorious vision with the dawn of sin. But do not forget that "Jesus came to restore creation to the purity of its origins" (CCC 2336). This will not be complete until heaven, yet through the gift of redemption, we can begin to reclaim what was lost even in this life.

The Spousal Meaning of the Body

Since lust so often holds sway in our fallen world, nakedness is often intertwined with all that is not holy. But in the beginning, John Paul says it was nakedness that revealed God's holiness in the visible world. God's holiness is his eternal mystery of self-giving love—the "exchange of love" between Father, Son, and Holy Spirit. Human holiness, in turn, is what enables "man to express himself deeply with his own body ... precisely through of the 'sincere gift' of self" (TOB 19:5).

Here the Pope draws from another favorite passage from Vatican II: "Man can fully discover his true self only in a sincere giving of himself" (GS 24). In other words, we can only discover "who we are" by loving as God loves. This, of course, is Christ's new commandment: "Love one another as I have loved you" (John 15:12). How did Christ love us? Recall his words at the Last Supper: "*This is my body which is given for you*" (Luke 22:19). Love is supremely spiritual, but as Christ demonstrates, love is expressed and realized *in the body.* In fact, God inscribed the call to divine love in our bodies—in our sexuality—right from the beginning.

In their nakedness, the first man and woman discovered what the Pope calls "the spousal meaning of the body." Spousal love (we could also say marital, nuptial, or conjugal love) is the love of *total self-donation.* The spousal meaning of the body, therefore, is the body's *"power to express love: precisely that love in which the human person becomes a gift* and— through this gift—fulfills the very meaning of his being and existence" (TOB 15:1).

If you are looking for the meaning of life, according to John Paul II, it is impressed right in your body—in human sexuality. The purpose of life is to love as God loves, and this is what your body as a man or woman is meant for. There is an intelligibility to the male and female body. Seen in light of the male-female pair, sexual difference reveals the unmistakable plan of God that man and woman are meant to be a "gift" to one another. Not only that, but their mutual gift (in the normal course of events) leads to a "third." As John Paul expresses it, "knowledge" leads to generation: "Adam *knew* his wife and she conceived" (Genesis 4:1).

Fatherhood and motherhood "crown" and completely reveal the mystery of sexuality. God's first directive in Genesis, "Be fruitful and multiply" (Genesis 1:28), is not merely an injunction to propagate. It is a call to love in God's image and thus "fulfill the very meaning of our being and existence."

The Fundamental Element of Existence

Marriage and procreation, of course, are not the only ways to "love as God loves." They serve as the original model, but whenever we imitate Christ in "giving up our bodies" for others, we express the body's spousal meaning. Christ, in fact, will call some to sacrifice marriage "for the sake of the kingdom" (see Matthew 19:12). As we will see more clearly in chapter five, celibacy for the kingdom *is not a rejection of sexuality.* It is a call to embrace *the ultimate meaning and purpose of sexuality.* The "one flesh" union is only a foreshadowing of something infinitely more grand

and glorious—the eternal union of Christ and the Church (see Ephesians 5:31-32). Again, this will be clearer later on, but those who choose the charism of celibacy forego marriage to devote themselves to follow the call of Christ in a particular way.

Whatever our particular vocation, we are all called to participate in God's love and share it with others. When we have the purity to see it, this is what the human body and human sexuality teach us. The spousal meaning of the body (that is, the call to love that God inscribed in our flesh) reveals what Vatican II describes as "the universal call to holiness" (see LG, chapter 5). And yet how many people spurn their bodies and their sexuality in the name of a supposed holiness? The spousal meaning of the body "is the fundamental component of human existence in the world" (TOB 15:5). We dare not spurn this! The more we grow in authentic (that is, embodied) holiness, the more we "discover and strengthen the bond that exists between the dignity of the human being (of the man or the woman) and the spousal meaning of his body" (TOB 86:8).

How do we grow in authentic, embodied holiness? How do we begin to reclaim something of the happiness and peace experienced by the first man and woman? The Pope examines this in his next cycle of reflections.

Chapter 3

THE ENTRANCE OF THE FIG LEAVES: THE EFFECTS OF SIN AND THE REDEMPTION OF THE BODY

*In the Sermon on the Mount "the Spirit of the
Lord gives new form to our desires, those inner
movements that animate our lives."*
                                        – CCC 2764

In his second cycle of reflections, the Pope contemplates the sexual and bodily experiences of "historical" men and women. History, in this sense, begins with the entrance of the fig leaves—that is, with the dawn of sin (see Genesis 3:7-10). But, as historical men and women, we are not only affected by sin; we are also redeemed in Christ. We must always balance the "bad news" of sin with the "good news" of redemption.

The bad news, as this chapter will discuss in more detail, is that we have fallen from the purity of our origins. The good news we will unfold is that "Jesus came to restore creation to the purity of its origins" (CCC 2336). As stated earlier, we cannot return to the state of innocence, but by the power of Christ's death and resurrection, we can progress more significantly on the journey of restoration than most people imagine. This can be a "messy" journey. Yet even though the fullness of redemption is reserved for heaven, our flat tires really can regain a significant amount of air even here on earth.

Adultery in the Heart

Once again, the Pope bases his reflections on Christ's words, this time from the Sermon on the Mount: "You have heard that it was said, 'You shall not commit adultery.' But I say to you that everyone who looks at a woman lustfully has already committed adultery with her in his heart" (Matthew 5:27-28).

For the sake of example, Christ speaks directly of male lust, but the principle applies equally to women. Most would agree that male lust seems geared more toward physical gratification at the expense of a woman, while female lust seems geared more toward emotional gratification at the expense of a man. Of course, this is not always the case. Women have physical cravings just as men have emotional ones. But the saying that "men will use love in order to get sex and women will use sex in order to feel loved" rings true at some level.

We can also observe that some people experience lust for the same sex. Homosexuality is a complex issue that we cannot discuss at length here. (For a more detailed discussion, see chapter eight of my book *Good News About Sex and Marriage*.) In short, while there is a strong push today to normalize homosexuality, in reality it is another manifestation of "flat-tire syndrome." No matter what our particular experience of lust, we are all in need of "re-inflation." The good news of the Gospel is that, if we take up our crosses and follow him, Christ can empower all of us to live in accord with God's wise design for creating us male and female. No one—no matter what his or her distortions—is beyond the scope of Christ's redeeming love.

When Christ speaks of "looking with lust," he is not saying that a mere glance or momentary thought makes us guilty of adultery. As fallen human beings, we will always be able to sense the "pull" of lust in our hearts and in our bodies. This doesn't mean we have sinned. It is what we do when we experience the pull of lust that matters. Do we seek God's help in resisting it or do we indulge it? When we indulge it—that is, when we actively choose "in our hearts" to treat another person as merely an object for our own gratification—we seriously violate that person's dignity and our own. We are meant to be loved "for our own sakes," never used as an object for someone else's sake. For John Paul II, the opposite of love is not hatred; rather, the opposite of love is to *use* someone as a means to our own selfish ends.

Furthermore, it is significant that Christ refers to looking lustfully at "a woman" in the generic sense. He doesn't stress that it is someone other than a spouse. As John Paul observes, a man commits "adultery in the heart" not only by looking lustfully at a woman he is not married to, "but *precisely because he looks in this way at a woman. Even* if he were to look in this way at ... his wife, he would commit the same adultery 'in the heart'" (TOB 43:2). In other words, marriage does *not* justify lust. It doesn't make *using* your spouse OK. I know this is a cliché, but why do so many wives claim to have a "headache" when their husbands want to have sex? If a woman is being *used* by her husband, it is totally understandable for her to recoil. The sexual embrace is meant to image and express divine love. Anything less is a counterfeit that not only fails to satisfy, but it can wound us terribly.

Words of Salvation, Not Condemnation

The Pope acknowledges that Christ's words about lust are severe. But he asks, are we to fear the severity of these words, or rather have confidence in their power to save us (see TOB 43:7)? These words have power to save us because the one who speaks them is the "Lamb of God who takes away the sin of the world" (John 1:29). Most people see in Christ's words only a condemnation. Do we forget that Christ came into the world not to condemn but to save (see John 3:17)?

Christ's words about lust call us to "enter our full image" (see TOB 25:2). As part of the heritage of original sin, lust obscures in each of us God's original, beautiful plan for sexual love—but it has not snuffed it out. The Pope insists that the heritage of our hearts is *deeper* than lust, and if we are honest with ourselves, we still desire what is deeper. If the human heart is a deep well, it is true that murky waters abound. But if we press through the mud and the mire, at the bottom of the well we do not find grime and sludge. We find a spring that, when activated, gradually fills the well to overflowing with pure, living water. This spring is the "deeper heritage" of our hearts. John Paul II proclaims that the words of Christ reactivate that deeper heritage, giving it *real power* in our lives (see TOB 46:6).

This means that we needn't walk through life merely coping with our lusts and disorders. Christ didn't die on a cross and rise from the dead to give us more coping mechanisms for our sins. We already had plenty of those without a savior. Christ died on a cross and rose from the dead to save us from sin so that we, too, could live a new life (see Romans 6:4). Again, we need to stress that this "new life" will only come to fulfillment in the resurrection at the end of time; "but it is also true that, in a certain way, we have already risen with Christ" (CCC 1002). Here and now we can begin to experience the redemption of our sexual desires, the gradual transformation of our hearts. It is a difficult and even arduous journey, but one that can be accomplished.

Questioning God's Gift

If we are to experience the redemption of our sexuality, we must first examine how and why we fell from God's original plan for it. So, once again, John Paul II takes us back to Genesis, this time to examine the nature of the original sin and the entrance of the fig leaves.

The Pope describes original sin as "the questioning of the gift." Allow me to explain. The deepest yearning of the human heart is to be "like God" by sharing in his life and love. Right from the beginning, God had granted man and woman a sharing in his own life and love as a totally free gift. Using the spousal image, God *initiated* the gift of himself as "bridegroom," and man (male and female) opened to *receive* the gift as "bride." In turn, man and woman were able to re-image this same "exchange of love" through their own marital self-giving and unity.

In order to retain this divine likeness and remain in his love, God had only asked that they not eat from "the tree of the knowledge of good and evil." If they did eat of it, they would cut themselves off from the source of life and love. In other words, they would die (see Genesis 2:16-17).

Sounds simple enough. So where did it all go wrong? "Behind the disobedient choice of our first parents lurks a seductive voice, opposed to God, which makes them fall into death out of envy. Scripture and the Church's Tradition see in this being a fallen angel, called 'Satan' or the 'devil'" (CCC 391). As we observed in the first chapter, Satan's no dummy. He knows that God created the union of the sexes as a sharing in divine life, and his goal is to keep us from this. So he aims his attack at *"the very heart of that unity that had from the 'beginning,' been formed by man and woman,* created and called to become 'one flesh'" (TOB 20:1).

Having approached the woman—the one who represents us all as "bride" in our *receptivity* to God's gift— the serpent insists, "You will not die [if you eat from the forbidden tree]. For God knows that when you eat of it your eyes will be opened, and you will be like God, knowing good and evil" (Genesis 3:4-5). We might read the serpent's temptation like this: "God doesn't love you. He is not looking out for you. He is a tyrant, a slave-driver who wants to keep you from what you really want. That is why he told you not to eat from that tree. If you want life and happiness, if you want to be 'like God,' then you have to reach out and grasp it for yourself because God sure won't give it to you."

Herein lies the *questioning*—and, ultimately, the denial—of God's gift. In the moment they reject their *receptivity* before God and *grasp* at their own "happiness," they turn their backs on God's love, on God's gift. In a way, they cast God's love out of their hearts. "Then the eyes of both were opened, and they knew that they were naked; and they sewed fig leaves together and made themselves aprons" (Genesis 3:7).

The tendency to "grasp" seems built-in to our fallen nature. We can observe it even in little children. For example, when my son asks for a cookie for dessert, before

I can even get the cookie out of the box to present it to him as a gift, what does he do? He *grasps* at it. So, taking advantage of this teachable moment, I might say to him, "Thomas, you are denying the gift. Your Papa loves you. I want to *give* this cookie to you as a gift. If you believed in the gift, all you would need to do is hold your hands out in confidence and *receive* the cookie as a gift." This is the problem with us all. We do not trust enough in our Father's love, so we grasp at happiness.

The Second Discovery of Sex

God said if they ate from the tree they would die. They didn't keel over dead, but they did die spiritually. In the act of creation, God had "in-spired" their bodies with his own life and love (see Genesis 2:7). Now their bodies "ex-spired" ("breathed-out") God's Spirit. Void of God's love, their desire for one another was altogether different. Having "denied the gift" in their relationship with God, they no longer experienced sexual desire as the power to be a gift to one another. Instead, they desired to *grasp* and *possess* one another for their own gratification. As John Paul says, with the dawn of lust, the *"relationship of the gift changes into a relationship of appropriation"* (TOB 32:6). To "appropriate" in this sense means "to take hold of" with the desire to *use*.

The Pope calls this "the second discovery of sex." In the "first" discovery of sex they experienced total peace and tranquility. Now they immediately felt "threatened." Nakedness originally revealed their God-like dignity. Now they instinctively hide their nakedness from the other's look.

Shame, therefore, has a double meaning. It indicates that they have lost sight of the spousal meaning of their bodies (God's plan of love stamped in their sexuality), but it also indicates an inherent need to *protect* the spousal meaning of the body from the degradation of lust. As the Pope poetically expresses it, lust "tramples on the ruins" of the spousal meaning of the body and aims directly to satisfy only the "sexual need" of the body (see TOB 40:4). It seeks "the sensation of sexuality" apart from a true gift of self and a true communion of persons. Lust, in fact, shatters their communion.

Lust is often thought of as some benefit to the sexual relationship or it is conceived of as an *increase* or *intensification* of sexual desire. In reality, lust is a *reduction* of the original fullness God intended for sexual desire. We do not get "more" when we lust but much less. Indulging in lust is comparable to eating out of a dumpster, when God invites us to the feast of eternal life. Why would we ever choose a dumpster? Because we do not really believe in the great gift of God's banquet. This is the gift man and woman denied with original sin. Shame, in turn, indicates our attraction toward the "dumpster."

In a way man and woman blame their bodies for lust. But such an approach is quite literally a "cover-up"—almost an "excuse" not to face the deep disorder of their hearts. As Jesus stresses in the Sermon on the Mount, lust is first and foremost a problem of the heart, not the body. Until we address the disordered desires of our hearts, we will never be able to live as the men and women God created us to be. As we observed previously, lust tends to affect the male and female personality differently, but the hearts of both men and women have become a battlefield between love and lust (see TOB 32:3).

Christian Ethos: Morality "from the Heart"

Conforming our behavior to an external norm is not enough. We all know it is possible to follow "the rules" without ever attaining holiness (that is, without a heart "in-spired" by God's love). This kind of rigid and lifeless conformity to rules is called "legalism" or "moralism." In the Sermon on the Mount, Christ calls us to something *very* different. He calls us to a "living morality" that flows from the heart.

Jesus sets the stage for this "new" morality by saying, "Unless your righteousness exceeds that of the scribes and the Pharisees, you will never enter the kingdom of heaven"

(Matthew 5:20). What could these words have sounded like to the Jews who heard them? The Scribes and the Pharisees were considered the most righteous of all. But for many of them, at least the ones Jesus singled out, it was all external. They conformed to the ethic, but their "ethos" remained skewed.

An *ethic* is an external norm or rule—"do this," "don't do that." *Ethos* refers to a person's inner-world of values, what attracts and repulses him deep in the heart. In the Sermon on the Mount, Christ is not only confirming God's ethical code. He is also proclaiming the true *ethos* of God's commandments—what they call us to *internally*. In effect Christ says, "You have heard the ethic not to commit adultery, but the problem is you *desire* to commit adultery. Your *ethos* is flawed because you're filled with lust."

It seems almost cruel. Knowing we are filled with lust, Jesus says, "Don't lust." Great! So what are we supposed to do? Christ holds out a standard he knows we cannot meet. It seems hopeless—*unless* ... unless it were possible to experience some kind of redemption or transformation of our desires. This is precisely where the Gospel becomes *good news*. As John Paul II repeatedly stresses, the "new ethos" that Christ proclaims in the Sermon on the Mount is not only given to us as a task. It is also given as a gift. We are not left to our own flaws, weaknesses, and sinfulness. In the "Sermon on the Mount ... the Spirit of the Lord gives new form to our desires, those inner movements that animate our lives" (CCC 2764).

As the Pope puts it, "Christian ethos is characterized by *a transformation of the human person's conscience and attitudes ... such as to express and realize the value of the body and sex* according to the Creator's original plan" (TOB 45:3). What good news! What hope! What joy! We are not *bound* by lust. The new dimension of *ethos* is always connected with the heart's liberation from lust (see TOB 43:6). As we are gradually loosed from the chains of lust, we are freed to love according to God's original plan. This is "a living morality," the Pope says, in which we realize the very meaning of our humanity (see TOB 24:3).

Freedom from the Law

Most people look at Christian morality—especially sexual morality—as an oppressive list of rules to follow. How far this misunderstanding is from the "living morality" proclaimed by Christ! The Gospel doesn't give us more rules to follow. The Gospel is meant to *change our hearts* so that we no longer need the rules (see CCC 1968). To the degree that we experience this change of heart, we experience "freedom from the law" (see Romans 7; Galatians 5)—not freedom to break the law; freedom to *fulfill* it.

Here is an example of what freedom from the law looks like: Do you have any desire to murder your best friend? This may seem like an odd question, but it actually demonstrates the point. Assuming you do not, then you do not need the commandment "Thou shalt not murder thy best friend" because you have no desire to break it. To this extent you are "free from the law." In other words, you do not experience this law ("Thou shalt not murder thy best friend") as an imposition because your heart already conforms to it.

Before sin, the human heart conformed totally to God's will. For example, the first married couple did not need a law forbidding adultery. They had no desire to commit adultery (and not only because there was no one else around). Only with "flat-tire syndrome" do we experience a rupture between our desires and God's will for us. Here is where the law serves its essential purpose. It is given to convict us of sin (see Romans 7:7). However, when Christ says "You have heard the commandment ... but I tell you ..." he indicates that we need something more than mere precepts can offer.

The Old Testament law is good and just, but it "does not of itself give the strength, the grace of the Spirit, to fulfill it" (CCC 1963). In other words, it convicts us of "driving with flat tires," but it does not re-inflate those tires. "The Law of the Gospel," however, "proceeds to reform the heart, the root of human acts, where man chooses between the pure and the impure" (CCC 1968).

To the degree that we allow Christ to "re-inflate our tires," we no longer need the law because we no longer desire to break it. What laws do you still need? What teachings of the Church feel like a burden or imposition to you? Perhaps the problem is not with the law or with the Church, but with your own "hardness of heart." Don't throw away the law; surrender your disordered desires to Christ and let him transform them.

Trying to follow all the rules without seeking air for our flat tires is futile. Those who do will either become self-righteous hypocrites or they will abandon God's law for a rationalized, watered-down version of the Gospel. Either way it is a "gospel" without the good news; it is Christianity without Christ. Both the self-righteous and the lawless have yet to "pass-over" from the bondage of the ethical code to the freedom of the "new ethos"—the freedom of redemption.

Such freedom liberates us not from the *external* "constraint" that calls us to good, but from the *internal* constraint that hinders our choice of the good. When we *desire* what is true, good, and beautiful, then we are free indeed—free to love, free to bless, which is the freedom from the compulsion to *grasp* and *possess*. Those who toss off the law in order to indulge their lusts may imagine themselves free, but like an alcoholic who cannot say no to the bottle, a person who cannot say "no" to lust is *enslaved*. "For freedom Christ has set us free; stand fast therefore, and do not submit again to a yoke of slavery" (Galatians 5:1).

The Grace of Creation Becomes the Grace of Redemption

As John Paul says, living in this freedom "is a still uncertain and fragile journey as long as we are on earth, but it is one made possible by grace, which enables us to possess the full freedom of the children of God (see Romans 8:21)" (VS 18). We are not justified by the law. We are "justified by ... grace as a gift, through the redemption which is in Christ" (Romans 3:24).

What is *grace?* John Paul describes it as God's mysterious

gift to the human heart that enables men and women to live in the reciprocal and sincere gift of self (see TOB 16:3). In the beginning, man and woman were infused with grace. When they doubted God's love and "denied the gift," they fell from grace. If this is the source of the problem, what is the first step toward a solution? Faith. If original sin is our denial of God's gift, "*faith*, in its deepest essence, is *the openness* of the human heart to the gift: *to God's self-communication in the Holy Spirit*" (DV 51).

The Pope observes that when Christ calls us to overcome lust in the Sermon on the Mount, his words bear witness that the original grace of creation has become for each of us the grace of redemption (see TOB 46:5). The Son of God took on flesh and died on a cross so that our sinful humanity might be put to death. He rose from the dead to "re-create" our humanity. He ascended into heaven with his glorified body to "in-spire" our bodies once again with God's life and love. Through this gift of our redemption, Christ breathes back into our flesh that same Spirit (grace) that "ex-pired" from our bodies when we denied the gift (see John 20:22).

Repent and Believe in the Good News

Jesus' whole life bears witness to the truth we find so hard to believe: God loves us; he is unequivocally *for* us, not against us. The "banquet" really exists and everyone without exception is invited. The only "requirement" for entry is that we stop eating out of the dumpster.

In essence, Christ's life proclaims: "You don't believe God loves you? Let me show you how much God loves you. You don't believe that God is 'gift'? This is my body *given* for you (see Luke 22:19). You think God wants to keep you from life? I will offer myself so that my life's blood can give you life to the full (see John 10:10). You thought God was a tyrant, a slave-driver? I will take the form of a slave (see Philippians 2:7); I will let you 'lord it over' me to demonstrate that God has no desire to 'lord it over' you (see Matthew 20:28). You thought God would whip your back if you gave him the chance? I will let you whip my back to demonstrate that God has no desire to whip yours. I have not come to condemn you but to save you (see John 3:17). I have not come to enslave you but to set you free (see Galatians 5:1). Stop persisting in your unbelief. Repent and believe in the good news" (see Mark 1:15).

As we open ourselves to this gift, the grace of redemption begins to "re-vivify" our humanity, to enliven our hearts with God's own goodness. To the degree that we allow this grace to inform and *transform* us, the Holy Spirit impregnates our reciprocal relations "with everything that is noble and beautiful," with "the supreme value which is love" (TOB 46:5).

Where is the grace of redemption poured out? Primarily in the sacramental life of the Church. Sacraments are not merely religious rituals. They infuse holiness into the terrain of our humanity: they penetrate our soul and body, our femininity and masculinity, with the power of holiness (see TOB 117b:2). In other words, sacraments make Christ's death and resurrection a *living reality* in our own lives. Unfortunately, many Christians fail to tap into the power of the sacraments. Through baptism alone, it is as if we have been given a trillion dollars in our bank accounts, but few of us seem to withdraw more than about seventy-five cents. In the sacraments, God's love is "poured into our hearts through the Holy Spirit" (Romans 5:5). We need to "bank" on this gift.

Life in the Spirit and the Redemption of the Body

In St. Paul's terminology, living the life of grace is synonymous with living "according to the Spirit." He contrasts this with "living according to the flesh." Walk "by the Spirit, and do not gratify the desires of the flesh. For the desires of the flesh are against the Spirit, and the desires of the Spirit are against the flesh" (Galatians 5:16-17).

This does *not* mean, as many a Christian has tragically concluded, that St. Paul condemns the body or thinks of it as an inherent obstacle to living a "spiritual" life. As we have already learned in our study of the Pope's teaching, the body is the specific vehicle of the spiritual life. In this context, "the flesh" refers to the whole person (body and soul) cut off from God's "in-spiration," cut off from God's indwelling Spirit. It refers to a person dominated by lust and the other vices. In turn, the person who lives "according to the Spirit" does *not* reject his body, but opens his whole body-soul personality to divine "in-spiration."

With great hope, John Paul II proclaims that as much as lust enslaves us by disordering our passions, so much does this "life according to the Spirit" free us to be a gift to others. As much as lust blinds us to the truth of God's plan for the body, so much does "life according to the Spirit" open our eyes to the body's spousal meaning (see TOB 101:5). So, to the degree that we open ourselves to "life in the Spirit" we also experience the "redemption of our bodies" (Romans 8:23).

John Paul II insists that "the redemption of the body" is not only a heavenly reality. We await its fulfillment then, but it is already at work in us now. This means that as we allow our lusts to be "crucified with Christ" (see Galatians 5:24), we can progressively rediscover in what is erotic that original "spousal meaning of the body" and live it. John Paul II says that this liberation from lust and the freedom it affords is, in fact, the condition for living all of life together in the truth (see 43:6).

Purity Is Not Prudishness

To the degree that we live the redemption of our bodies, we understand that sexual purity is not a matter of annihilating or repressing sexual attraction and desire. As Karol Wojtyla, the future Pope John Paul II, wrote in *Love and Responsibility*, mature purity "consists in quickness to affirm the value of the person in every situation, and in raising [sexual reactions] to the personal level" (LR, pp. 170-171). In the Sermon on the Mount, Christ is not simply saying "don't look." John Paul explains that Jesus' words are "an invitation to a pure way of looking at others, capable of respecting the spousal meaning of the body" (VS 15).

Obviously, if a person needs to turn away in order to avoid lusting, then, by all means, "don't look." For the person who is bound by lust, the Old Testament admonition, "Turn away your eyes from a shapely woman" (Sirach 9:8) retains all its wisdom. We classically call this "avoiding the occasion of sin" by "gaining custody of the eyes." This is a necessary first step, but the Pope would describe such an approach as a "negative" purity. As we grow in virtue we come to experience "positive" or "mature" purity. In mature purity we enjoy the fruits of the victory won over lust. We enjoy the "efficacy of the gift of the Holy Spirit" who restores to our experience of the body "all *its simplicity, its lucid clarity*, and also *its interior joy*" (TOB 58:7).

Practically everyone begins the journey towards mature purity on the "negative" side. Unfortunately, many people stagnate at this stage thinking it is all they can expect. Keep going! Needless to say, I am far from being a perfect man, but I can attest to the fact that as we appropriate the gift of redemption in our lives, lust loses sway in our hearts. We come not only to understand, but to *see* and *experience* the body as a "theology," a sign of God's own mystery. "Blessed are the pure in heart, for they shall see God" (Matthew 5:8). If we understand what the Pope is holding out to us here, we can add: "Blessed are the pure in heart, for they shall see God's mystery revealed through the body."

Purity, therefore, is not prudishness. It does *not* reject the body. "Purity is the glory of the human body before God. It is the glory of God in the human body, through which masculinity and femininity are manifested" (TOB 57:3). Purity in its fullness will only be restored in heaven. Yet, as the *Catechism* teaches, "Even now [purity of heart] enables us to see *according to* God ... it lets us perceive the human body—ours and our neighbor's—as a temple of the Holy Spirit, a manifestation of divine beauty" (CCC 2519).

We have to reckon with the fact that we have a Pope who, in the restoration of the Sistine Chapel, ordered the removal of several loincloths that previous popes had painted over Michelangelo's original nudes. He did this in the name of Christian purity. During the homily dedicating the restored frescos, John Paul proclaimed the Sistine Chapel *"the sanctuary of the theology of the human body."* He added, "It seems that Michelangelo, in his own way, allowed himself to be guided by the evocative words of the Book of Genesis which ... reveals: 'The man and his wife were both naked, yet felt no shame' (Genesis 2:25)" (April 13, 1994).

What, then, is the difference between pornography and a proper artistic portrayal of nakedness? The Pope says the difference lies in the intention of the artist. Pornographic portrayals of the body raise objection "not because of their object, because in itself the human body always has its own inalienable dignity—but because of the quality or way of its artistic reproduction" (TOB 63:5). The pornographer seeks only to arouse lust in the viewer, while the true artist (such as Michelangelo) helps us see "the whole personal mystery of man." Proper portrayals of the naked body can teach us "the spousal meaning of the body which corresponds to, and provides the measure for 'purity of heart'" (TOB 63:5). Those who experience mature purity understand the naked body for what it is—the revelation of God's plan of love.

The Interpretation of Suspicion

Doubters respond, "Impossible! The naked body will always arouse lust." For the person dominated by lust, this is true. But, applying one of the Pope's boldest declarations of redemption, "of which man are we speaking? Of man *dominated* by lust or of man *redeemed by Christ?* This is what is at stake: the *reality* of Christ's redemption. *Christ has redeemed us!* This means he has given us the possibility of realizing the *entire truth* of our being; he has set our freedom free from the *domination* of lust" (VS 103).

As Karol Wojtyla wrote in *Love and Responsibility*, we cannot simply equate nakedness with immodesty and lust. Immodesty is certainly present "when nakedness plays a negative role with regard to the value of the person, when its aim is to arouse [lust]." But, Wojtyla adds, "this is not inevitable" (LR, 190-191). If we think a "lustful look" is the only way a person *can* look at the human body, then we subscribe to what John Paul II calls "the interpretation of suspicion." Those who live by suspicion remain so locked in their own lusts that they project the same bondage on to everyone else. They cannot imagine any way to think about the human body and the sexual relationship other than through the prism of lust.

When we hold the human heart in "a state of continual and irreversible suspicion" (TOB 46:4) because of lust, we condemn ourselves to a hopeless, loveless existence. We condemn ourselves to following the rules (*ethics*) without a change of heart (*ethos*). Eventually, we abandon God's law because we simply cannot keep it. This kind of permanent suspicion effectively cuts us off from the *power* of the Gospel.

As St. Paul warns us, we must avoid the trap of "holding the form of religion" while "denying the power of it" (2 Timothy 3:5). "Redemption is a truth, a reality, in the name of which man must feel called, and 'called with effectiveness'" (TOB 46:4). In other words, the death and resurrection of Christ is *effective.* It can change our lives, our attitudes, our hearts—yes—our sexual desires. *"Do not empty the cross of its power!"* (see 1 Corinthians 1:17). John Paul exclaims that this "is the cry of the new evangelization" (OL 3).

Much is at stake. "The meaning of life is the antithesis of the [interpretation] 'of suspicion.'" This interpretation "is very different, *it is radically different* from the one we discover *in Christ's words* in the Sermon on the Mount. These words bring to light ... another vision of man's possibilities" (TOB 46:6). Unless we tap into this "other vision of man's possibilities," we will find it impossible to love as Christ loves; we will remain cut off from the meaning of life.

Growing in Mature Purity

So how do we tap into this "other vision of man's possibilities"? How do we progress from "negative" purity to "positive"? I will begin with a quote from the Pope and then add some personal reflections.

To grow in purity, the Pope says we most devote ourselves to "a progressive education in self-control of the will, of sentiments, of emotions, which must be developed from the simplest gestures, in which it is relatively easy to put the inner decision into practice" (TOB 128:1). For example, what are your eating habits? If you cannot say no to a potato chip, how are you going to say no to indulging in lust? Fasting is a wonderful way to grow in mastery of our passions. If this is not already part of your life, start with a simple sacrifice that is relatively easy to put into practice. As you continue exercising this "muscle," you will find your strength increasing. What was once "impossible" gradually becomes possible.

The muscle analogy, however, is only half right. Growing in purity certainly demands human effort, but we are also aided by supernatural grace. Here it is crucial to distinguish between indulgence, repression, and redemption. When lust "flares up," most people think they only have two choices: indulge or repress. If these are the only options, which one looks more "holy"? Repression. Yet there is another way! Rather than repressing lust by pushing it into the subconscious, trying to ignore it, or otherwise seeking to annihilate it, we must *surrender* our lusts to Christ and allow him to slay them. As we do, "the Spirit of the Lord gives new form to our desires" (CCC 2764). In other words, as we allow lust to be "crucified," we also come to experience the "resurrection" of God's original plan for sexual desire. Not immediately, but gradually, progressively, as we take up our cross every day and follow, we come to experience sexual desire as the power to love in God's image.

This process of transformation requires not only a resolute will but also a firm faith. It is the Holy Spirit who transforms our hearts, who "re-inflates our tires." And faith, you may recall, is the openness of the human heart to God's gift of the Holy Spirit (see DV 51).

When lust tempts you, or even overwhelms you, you might say a prayer like this: *Lord, I thank you for the gift of my sexual desires. I surrender this lustful desire to you and I ask you please, by the power of your death and resurrection, to "untwist" in me what sin has twisted so that I might experience the tranformation of sexual desire as you intend—as the desire to love in your image.*

To reinforce your decision to "die" to lust, you may also want to place yourself in the shape of a cross—hands outstretched—while repeating the above prayer. The point here is to conform yourself to Christ, to carry "in the body the death of Jesus, so that the life of Jesus may also be manifested in your bodies" (2 Corinthians 4:10).

Resolving *not* to indulge lust can be very difficult, at times even emotionally and physically wrenching. It seems few men and women experience the freedom for which Christ has set us free because when they taste this kind of "crucifixion," rather than staying the course which leads to resurrection, they "come down from the cross." When those nails are biting into your hands, and the burden of the cross seems too heavy to bear, keep going! You are on the verge of a passover from death to life, from lust to authentic love. Only if we are willing to die with Christ can we also live the resurrected life he offers.

Discerning the Movements of Our Hearts

Let me emphasize—if this is not clear enough already—that the "positive" approach to purity I am outlining with the Pope's help does not provide a license to "push the envelope." The person who uses anything in this book as an excuse to indulge his (or her) lusts is not seeking purity. Honest people know their limits. They know what situations would make them stumble and avoid them with the seriousness Christ demands of us. "If your right eye causes you to sin, pluck it out ... if your right hand causes you to sin, cut it off" (Matthew 5:29-30). Modern adaptation: "If your computer causes you to sin, throw it away. If your TV causes you to sin, get rid of it."

It is true that sometimes love and lust are difficult to distinguish. A man, for example, upon recognizing a woman's beauty, might wonder where the line is between seeing her as an object for his own gratification and loving her rightly as a person made in God's image. As John Paul writes, lust "is not always plain and obvious; sometimes it is concealed, so that it passes itself off as 'love'.... Does this mean that we should distrust the human heart? No!" the Pope insists. "It is only to say that we must remain in control of it" (TOB 32:3).

"Control" here doesn't mean merely dominating unruly desires in order to keep them "in check." Again, that is only the "negative" side of the picture. As we mature in self-control, we experience it as "*the ability to orient* [sexual] reactions, both as to their content and as to their character" (TOB 129:5). The person who is truly master of himself is able to direct erotic desire "toward what is true, good, and beautiful, so that what is 'erotic' also becomes true, good, and beautiful" (TOB 48:1). As this happens we come to understand and experience the mystery of sexuality "in a depth, simplicity, and beauty hitherto altogether unknown" (TOB 117b:5).

To paraphrase a very insightful passage, the Pope points out that getting to this point demands "perseverance and consistency" in learning the meaning of our bodies, the meaning of our sexuality. We must learn this not only in the abstract (although this, too, is necessary), but above all in the interior reactions of our own "hearts." This is a "science," the Pope says, which cannot really be learned only from books, because it is a question here of deep knowledge of our interior life. Deep in the heart we learn to distinguish between what, on the one hand, composes the great riches of sexuality and sexual attraction, and what, on the other hand, bears only the sign of lust. And although these internal movements of the heart can sometimes be confused with one another, we have been called by Christ to acquire a mature and complete evaluation. And the Pope concludes, "It should be added that this task *can* be carried out and that it is truly worthy of man" (TOB 48:4).

Let's close this chapter with a prayer for purity.

Lord, help me to discern the movements of my heart. Help me to distinguish between the great riches of sexuality as you created it to be and the distortions of lust. I grant you permission, Lord, to slay my lusts. Take them. Crucify them so that I might come to experience the resurrection of sexual desire as you intend. Grant me a pure heart. Amen.

Chapter 4

BEYOND THE FIG LEAVES:
GOD'S ULTIMATE PLAN FOR THE BODY

*Those who respond to the wedding invitation "will rejoice one day
with the beloved, in a happiness and rapture that can never end."*
– CCC 1821

We have looked briefly at our origin before sin and
our history affected by sin yet redeemed in Christ. Now, in
order to have a total vision of what it means to be human,
we must look to our ultimate destiny when (assuming we say
"yes" to the divine plan) God will raise our bodies in glory.

Returning to our image of the deflated tires, our
destiny cannot be understood only as a return to the fully
"inflated" state of the beginning. In the resurrection we
enter into an entirely *new* dimension of human life "beyond
all understanding and description" (CCC 1027). Tires, you
might say, will give way to *flight.*

Heaven – A Bodily Experience

Many people have an erroneous "super-spiritual" view
of heaven. Such people tend to see the body as a shell that
they are anxious to get rid of. This is *not* the Christian view
of things. Christians conclude their Creed with a bold
proclamation: "I believe in the resurrection of the body and
life everlasting. Amen." The *Catechism* observes, "'On no
point does the Christian faith meet with more opposition
than on the resurrection of the body.' It is very commonly
accepted that the life of the human person continues in a
spiritual fashion after death. But how can we believe that
this body, so clearly mortal, could rise to everlasting life"

51

(CCC 996)? What a mystery! In Christ "the mortal puts on immortality" (1 Corinthians 15:54).

We often speak of the "souls" in heaven. When we buried my grandmother, I saw her body go into the ground, and I am confident that her soul is now enjoying some form of union with God. But the souls currently in heaven ("currently," of course, is a time-bound word that does not even apply to heaven) remain in a state of separation from the body until the resurrection of their bodies. It cannot be any other way for us as human beings: Since God created us as a union of body and soul, the separation of the two at death is entirely "unnatural." Our bodies will certainly be different in their resurrected state (recall that the disciples did not recognize Jesus after the resurrection [see Luke 24:15-16]), but we will still have them!

The difference is that our bodies will be perfectly "spiritualized" (see 1 Corinthians 15:44). Spiritualization means that "*the powers of the spirit will permeate the energies of the body*" (TOB 67:1). And because the "spirit" that will permeate our bodies is not only our own human, created spirits, but the divine, uncreated Holy Spirit, John Paul II speaks also of the "divinization" (making divine) of the body. In a way totally inaccessible to us now, we will participate, body and soul, "in the divine nature" (2 Peter 1:4).

Recall our earlier discussion of God's innermost secret: "God himself is an eternal exchange of love, Father, Son, and Holy Spirit, and he has destined us to share in that exchange" (CCC 221). This is what we mean by the "spiritualization" and "divinization" of the body. To the degree that creatures can, we will share—body and soul— in God's eternal exchange of love. And this "great mystery" is prefigured right from the beginning in man and woman's "exchange of love," that is, in and through their union in "one flesh."

So, many ask, will there be sex in heaven? It depends what we mean by the term. Sex is not first what people *do*. It is who people *are* as male or female. John Paul II mentions three times in his audience of December 2, 1981 (and on other occasions throughout this cycle) that we will be raised *as male and female.* So, in this sense, yes, the signs of masculinity and femininity associated with human sexuality will be manifest in heaven. But, as we will learn from Christ's words about the resurrection, the union of the sexes as we know it now will give way to an *infinitely greater* union. Those who are raised in glory will experience a bliss so far superior to earthly sexual union that our wee brains cannot even begin to imagine it. Eye has not seen, ear has not heard, nor has it even dawned on us what God has prepared for those who love him (see 1 Corinthians 2:9).

Christ Points Us to the Ultimate "Marriage"

In his discussion with the Pharisees, Christ called men and women of history to look to "the beginning" in order to understand God's original plan for the sexual relationship. In his discussion with the Sadducees, Christ points us to an entirely new dimension of human sexuality and our call to union when he says that "in the resurrection they neither marry nor are given in marriage" (Matthew 22:30). These words form the basis of John Paul II's reflections on the destiny of man and woman.

At first glance, Christ's words may seem to undermine all we have said about the greatness of marital love and the sexual embrace. But examined more closely, these words point to the crowning glory of all we have said. Marriage and the "one flesh" union exist from the beginning to point us to the "marriage of the Lamb" (Revelation 19:7), to the union of Christ and the Church (see Ephesians 5:31-32). In the resurrection, the "primordial sacrament" will give way to the divine reality. In other words, if God created the union of the sexes as a foreshadowing of heaven, Christ is saying, "You no longer need a foreshadowing to point you *to* heaven when you are *in* heaven. You're there. The ultimate union has come."

People often ask, "Does this mean I won't be with my spouse in heaven?" Assuming you both say "yes" to God's wedding invitation, you will certainly be together. All who respond will live "together" in a communion that fulfills superabundantly all that is good, true, and beautiful about marriage and family life here on earth. What we need to understand is that the union of the sexes, as beautiful and wonderful as it is, is not our be-all and end-all. It is only an "icon," a sign of something infinitely greater. Paraphrasing the Holy Father, marriage does not express definitively the deepest meaning of sexuality. It merely provides a concrete expression of that meaning within history (see TOB 69:4). At the end of history, the "historical" expression of sexuality will make way for an entirely new expression of our call to life-giving communion.

Icons and Idols

When we lose sight of that infinitely greater union, we inevitably treat the icon as an idol. In other words, when we lose sight of the joys of heaven we tend to view sexual union and its physical pleasures as our ultimate fulfillment. Welcome to the world in which we live.

Still, there is an important element of truth in our society's idolatrous obsession with sex. Behind every false god we discover our desire for the true God gone awry. The sexual confusion so prevalent in our world and in our own hearts is simply the human desire for heaven gone berserk. Untwist the distortions and we discover the astounding glory of sex in the divine plan. "For this reason ... the two become one flesh." For what reason? To reveal, proclaim, and anticipate the eternal union of Christ and the Church (see Ephesians 5:31-32).

God gave us sexual desire, you might say, as the fuel of a rocket that is meant to launch us into the stars and beyond. Yet, what would happen if the engines of that rocket became inverted, pointing us back only upon ourselves and no longer toward the stars? Launch that rocket and the result is a massive blast of self-destruction. Herein we discover the importance of Christ's words about the new state of the body and sex in the resurrection: They help us set our sights on the union that alone can satisfy. When we let the "power" of these words sink into our hearts, they redirect our rocket engines toward the stars. The idol once again becomes the icon it was meant to be.

Only when our engines are pointed toward the stars does marriage take on its true meaning as a sacrament. Sacraments, when properly lived, give us a taste of heaven on earth. But when heaven comes, the sacraments, having served their purpose, give way. There will be no sacraments in heaven (see CCC 671), not because sacraments are annihilated, but because they are superabundantly fulfilled. Hence, the fact that we no longer marry in the resurrection should not cause sadness but rejoicing. Every human longing, every desire of the heart for love and union will be fulfilled beyond our wildest dreams. That deep "ache" of solitude will finally be completely and eternally satisfied.

Experience attests that even the most wonderful marriage does not fully satisfy our hunger for love and union. We still yearn for "something more." I love my wife, Wendy, more than any words can express, but she will not mind my saying that she is not my ultimate fulfillment. Do not hang your hat on a hook that cannot bear the weight! If we look to another human person as our ultimate fulfillment, we will crush that person. Only the eternal, ecstatic, "marriage" of heaven—so far superior to anything proper to earthly life that we cannot begin to fathom it—can satisfy the human "ache" of solitude.

The Beatific Vision

There are clear and important distinctions between our original, historical, and ultimate existence, but there is also a continuity. In short, if our origin and our history revolve around the "great mystery" of divine love and spousal communion, then our heavenly existence will revolve around the same, albeit in an entirely new dimension. Now we see dimly, as in a mirror, but then we will behold the Mystery "face to face" (see 1 Corinthians 13:12).

"Because of his transcendence, God cannot be seen as he is, unless he himself opens up his mystery to man's immediate contemplation and gives him the capacity for it.

The Church calls this contemplation of God in his heavenly glory 'the beatific vision'" (CCC 1028). "Beatify" means to make supremely happy. The unsurpassed beauty and splendor of the eternal vision of God will fill all who behold with never-ending bliss.

Recall man and woman's original "face-to-face" vision of each other. This provides a faint glimmer or prefigurement of the beatific vision. As John Paul says, man and woman experienced a "beatifying immunity from shame" in their nakedness precisely because their vision was infused with love. "Happiness is being rooted in love," the Pope affirms (TOB 16:3). Man and woman had no fear of being fully "seen" by the other because each loved and received the other in the full truth of his or her naked humanity. Their mutual vision expressed their profound, personal "knowledge" of each other. They "participated" in the sheer goodness of each other's humanity.

John Paul writes that the beatific vision of heaven is "a concentration of knowledge ... and love on God himself." This knowledge "cannot be anything but full participation in God's inner life, that is, in trinitarian Reality itself" (TOB 68:4). In the beatific vision we will *know* God and he will *know* us (he already does, of course). We will *participate* "fully" in God's divinity and he will *participate* fully in our humanity (he already does, of course, having taken on human nature in the Incarnation).

God has humbled himself to share in our humanity so that we might share in his own divine life. What a glorious exchange! As the *Catechism* says, the "Son of God became man so that we might become God" (CCC 460), so that we might participate in the divine nature (see 2 Peter 1:4). This, of course, does not mean that we will lose our human nature and become on par with God. It does mean, though, that God will give us a share in his own divinity, to the degree that our humanity will allow.

This divine-human exchange expresses something of the "content" or inner dynamic of the beatific vision. Recall here that this is exactly what the serpent convinced us God was withholding—his divine life and our happiness. "If you want to be 'like God,'" he insinuated "you need to *grasp* it." No! God has always desired for us to share fully in his own divinity. It is a free gift. All we need do is open to *receive* it. We need not grasp at what God freely gives us. Sin—and all human misery—begins right here, with grasping at the gift.

Fulfillment of the Spousal Meaning of the Body

How will this glorious exchange between God and man take place? Since the "nuptials" of heaven are beyond all human knowledge, all we can do is speculate. Yet, once again, we see a faint glimmer of what is to come in the nuptials of earth.

The original exchange of man and woman took place through the "freedom of the gift" and the "spousal meaning of the body." Recall that God gave us freedom as the capacity to love, as the capacity to make a "sincere gift" of ourselves to one another. "Man can only find himself through the sincere gift of self" (GS 24). Furthermore, God inscribed this call to self-donation right in our bodies as male and female. Our bodies have a "spousal meaning" because they are capable of expressing divine love, *"precisely that love in which the person becomes a gift* and—through this gift—fulfills the very meaning of his being and existence" (TOB 15:1).

Paraphrasing John Paul II, in the resurrection we discover—in a new, heavenly dimension—the same spousal meaning of the body. This time, however, the spousal meaning of the body is fulfilled in our meeting with the mystery of the living God, through our vision of him "face to face" (see TOB 67:5). The Pope does not elaborate, but applying the spousal analogy, we can conclude that in the resurrection, the divine Bridegroom will express his gift ("this is my body given for you") in its fullest reality. All who respond to the wedding invitation will open to receive this gift as Christ's bride. In response to this gift, we will give ourselves totally to the divine Bridegroom in an eternally life-giving embrace.

As the *Catechism* states, the Church "longs to be united

with Christ, her Bridegroom, in the glory of heaven" where she "will rejoice one day with [her] Beloved, in a happiness and rapture that can never end" (CCC 1821). John Paul writes that in this heavenly reality "penetration and permeation of what is essentially human by what is essentially divine will then reach its peak" (TOB 67:3).

The spousal imagery is unmistakable. Of course, when using spousal union as an image of heaven, it is more important than ever to remember the inadequacy of analogies. Caution is necessary. Heaven is not some eternally magnified experience of sexual union on earth. As John Paul II observes, the union to come "will be a completely new experience." Yet "at the same time," he says, "it will not be alienated in any way" from the love that man and woman experienced in "the beginning" and have sought to reclaim throughout history (see TOB 69:5). The original meaning of the body will then be revealed again in such *simplicity and splendor* when all who respond to the wedding invitation will live in the full freedom of self-giving love (see TOB 69:6). Those who rise to eternal life will experience "the absolute and eternal spousal meaning of the glorified body ... in union with God himself" (TOB 75:1).

The Communion of Saints

We will live this self-giving love not only as individuals in union with God. As alluded to earlier, we will also live in self-giving love and communion with all the saints who enjoy the beatific vision. Recall that, in his experience of solitude, Adam discovered his fundamental vocation: love of God *and* love of neighbor. Heaven fulfills both dimensions of this vocation. When we reach our ultimate destiny we will live in consummate union with all who are raised in glory.

"*For man*, this consummation will be the final realization of the unity of the human race, which God willed from creation. ... Those who are united with Christ will form the community of the redeemed, 'the holy city' of God, 'the Bride, the wife of the Lamb'" (CCC 1045). What was "the unity of the human race which God willed from creation"?

It was the unity of the two, male and female, in "one body" (Genesis 2:24). In the communion of saints there are "many parts" (a great multitude of glorified men and women), yet all are united eternally in "one body" (see 1 Corinthians 12:20).

This obviously will not be experienced in the sexual sense lived here on earth. Yet, we can conclude that in some mysterious way beyond earthly comprehension, all that is masculine in our humanity will be in union with all that is feminine in our humanity. That unity—that "one body"— will be the one Bride of Christ living in consummate union with her Bridegroom for eternity. In and through this communion with Christ, the communion of saints will live in communion with *the* Communion, the Trinity. We will *see* all and *be seen* by all. We will *know* all and *be known* by all— and God will be "all in all" (Ephesians 1:23).

As if it needs to be said again, *this* is the purpose of sexual union in the divine plan: to prefigure in some way the glory, ecstasy, and bliss that awaits us in heaven (see Ephesians 5:31-32). As the *Catechism* expresses it, "In the joys of their love [God gives spouses] here on earth a foretaste of the wedding feast of the Lamb" (CCC 1642).

No wonder we are all so darned interested in sex. God put an innate desire in every human being to want to understand it. Why? To lead us to him. But beware of the counterfeits! Because sex is meant to launch us toward heaven, the devil attacks right here. When our innate "curiosity" about sex is not met with the "great mystery" of the divine plan, we inevitably fall, in one way or another, for the counter-plan. In other words, when our desire to understand the body and sexuality is not met with the truth, we inevitably fall for the lies.

Our God Is Rich in Mercy

If you have fed your curiosity about sex with lies, do not despair. Our God is rich in mercy. Why was Christ so compassionate toward sinners? Think of the woman caught in adultery (see John 8:2-11). She went looking for love, intimacy, union with another, but, as always, the counterfeit could not satisfy. Laden with shame, she was brought before Christ by an angry crowd anxious to stone her. Christ then said whoever was without sin could cast the first stone. According to his own words, the sinless Christ could have thrown a stone, but Christ came not to condemn. He came to save (see John 3:17).

St. John writes that "Jesus was left alone with the woman standing before him" (John 8:9). Reading into the story a bit, we can imagine that in the woman's encounter with the divine Bridegroom she had a conversion from the counterfeit to the real thing. Do you think when Jesus said, "Go, and do not sin again" (John 8:11), that she turned and grumbled, "Who is this man to tell me what I can and cannot do with my body!"? Or do you think, having encountered the love she was truly looking for, she left transformed, renewed, affirmed in the deepest part of her being as a woman? This is what Christ offers to us all!

What are the lies you have believed? What are the counterfeits you have bought into? Behind them all is your authentic thirst for love. Sexual sin is a quest to satisfy that thirst with a tonic that never can. Christ meets us right there without condemnation. As he said to another sexual sinner in just such a meeting, "If you knew the gift of God ... you would have asked him and he would have given you living water" (John 4:10). Sin denies the gift. Faith opens to receive it and is satisfied.

Be not afraid! Invite Christ to sanctify your sexuality through the life of virtue. Christ *never* robs us of our humanity. He fully reveals it to us: "Christ, by the revelation of the mystery of the Father and his love, fully reveals man to himself and makes his supreme calling clear" (GS 22). What is that "supreme calling"? Here is the theological answer: Our supreme calling is to be part of the communion of saints, who participate in communion with Christ in the Communion of the Trinity. Here is the translation: Our supreme calling is eternal ecstasy; unrivaled rapture; bounteous, beauteous bliss.

Lord, grant us faith. Help us believe in this glorious gift. Amen.

Chapter 5

CELIBACY FOR THE KINGDOM: A MARRIAGE MADE IN HEAVEN

Celibacy for the kingdom signifies "the risen man, in [whom] the absolute and eternal spousal meaning of the glorified body will be revealed in union with God himself."
— John Paul II (TOB 75:1)

We have looked briefly at our origin, history, and destiny in order to answer the question "What does it mean to be human?" So, what *does* it mean? In brief, we have learned that to be human means we are called to *communion*—communion with God and with one another. As we learned at the end of the last chapter, this is a call to eternal ecstasy, unrivaled rapture, bounteous, beauteous bliss. We have also learned throughout that this call to communion with God and with all humanity is *stamped right in our bodies* as male and female.

We now shift gears in order to address the question "How can I live my life in a way that will bring true happiness?" In other words, returning to our favored image, once we have acquired some air in our tires, where should we drive the car? The Pope answers this question in terms of life vocation.

John Paul II writes: "Christian revelation recognizes two specific ways of realizing the vocation of the human person, in its entirety, to love: marriage and virginity or celibacy. Either one is in its own proper form an actuation of the most profound truth about man, of his being 'created in the image of God'" (FC 11). In this cycle, John Paul looks at the celibate vocation. Once again, he begins with the words of Christ.

Eunuchs "For the Kingdom"

When Jesus restored the permanence of marriage according to God's original plan, his disciples (like many today) concluded that it was better not to marry at all (see Matthew 19:10). In response to their contention, Jesus takes the discussion to a different plane altogether: "For there are eunuchs who have been so from birth, and there are eunuchs who have been made eunuchs by men, and there are eunuchs who have made themselves eunuchs for the sake of the kingdom of heaven" (Matthew 19:12).

In the Christian tradition, a eunuch "for the kingdom of heaven" is someone who freely forgoes sexual relations in anticipation of that state in which men and women "neither marry nor are given in marriage." Celibacy for the kingdom, therefore, "is a sign that the body, whose end is not the grave, is directed to glorification." It "is a testimony among men that anticipates the future resurrection" (TOB 75:1). In a sense, the celibate man or woman steps beyond the dimensions of history—while living within the dimensions of history—and proclaims to the world that "the kingdom of God is here"; the ultimate marriage has come.

Christian celibacy, therefore, is not a rejection of sexuality. It points us to the ultimate purpose and meaning of sexuality. "For this reason ... the two become one flesh." What reason does St. Paul give? Man and woman become one flesh as a sign or "sacrament" of Christ's eternal union with the Church (see Ephesians 5:31-32). Those who remain celibate for the kingdom forego the sacrament of marriage in anticipation of the heavenly reality, the "marriage of the Lamb." If it is "not good for man to be alone," Christian celibacy reveals that the ultimate fulfillment of solitude is found only in union with God. In a way, the celibate person freely chooses to remain in the "ache" of solitude in this life in order to devote all of his longings to the union that alone can satisfy.

The word "celibacy," unfortunately, does not usually convey this deeper meaning. It is a negative word in the sense that it tells us what these people are *not* doing.

"Eunuch" can even have worse connotations. Perhaps we would do better to define this vocation in terms of what it embraces and anticipates versus what it gives up. It embraces and anticipates "the heavenly marriage."

Celibacy Must Be Freely Chosen

A survey recently circulated among priests posed a question something like this: "Should celibacy be a free choice or should it continue to be *imposed by the Church*?" Contrary to widespread opinion, the Church forces *no one* to be celibate. Christ's words ("there are eunuchs who have *made themselves* eunuchs") "clearly indicate the importance of the personal choice" of this vocation (TOB 74:1). If someone were *forced* into celibacy, it would be no more legitimate than if someone were *forced* into marriage.

We tend to forget in the Latin Church that male celibacy is a vocation in itself, apart from priesthood. The Catholic and Orthodox Churches of the East not only have a valid married priesthood, they also have a vibrant non-ordained celibate brotherhood (this exists in the West as well, but is not as prominent). As the *Catechism* indicates, the Latin Church usually chooses her priests from among men of faith who have chosen celibacy as their life's vocation (see CCC 1579). This seems to imply that the choice of celibacy should come first. If a Catholic man (in the Western church) has discerned a celibate vocation, then, within his life of celibacy, he might also discern a call to priesthood. Those priests who believe celibacy was foisted on them, it seems, have not understood these important distinctions.

As a result, many today are clamoring for an end to priestly celibacy. Some even blame celibacy itself for the sexual problems and abuses of some of the clergy. As I wrote in my book *Good News About Sex and Marriage*, "Celibacy does not *cause* sexual disorder. Sin does. Simply getting married does not *cure* sexual disorder. Christ does. If a priest, or any other man, were to enter marriage with deep-seated sexual disorders, he would be condemning his wife to a life of sexual objectification. The only way the scandal of sexual sin (whether committed by priests or others) will end is if people experience the redemption of their sexuality in Christ" (GN, p. 163).

Authentic Christian celibacy witnesses dramatically to this redemption. It is true that, as a *discipline* of the Latin Church (rather than a doctrine), the practice of reserving priestly ordination to those men who have chosen a celibate life could change. But when we realize how celibacy points us to the ultimate meaning of sex, we recognize that our world needs the witness of Christian celibacy now more than ever.

Celibacy Flows from the Redemption of Sexuality

To a world bound by lust, life-long celibacy seems absurd. The world's general attitude towards Christian celibacy might be summarized like this: "Hey, marriage is the only 'legitimate' chance you Christians get to indulge your lusts. Why the heck would you ever want to give that up? You would be condemning yourself to a life of hopeless repression." But recall that indulgence and repression are not the only choices. There is another way unknown to the world (and sadly, unknown to many Christians as well). As we have already said, "Jesus came to restore creation to the purity of its origins" (CCC 2336).

The difference between marriage and celibacy must *never* be understood as the difference between having a "legitimate" outlet for sexual lust on the one hand and having to repress it on the other. Christ calls *everyone*— no matter his or her particular vocation—to experience redemption from the domination of lust. Only from this perspective do the Christian vocations (celibacy *and* marriage) make any sense. *Both* vocations—if they are to be lived as Christ intends—flow from the same experience of the redemption of sexual desire.

John Paul states that the celibate person must submit *"the sinfulness of his humanity to the powers that flow from the mystery of the redemption of the body* ... just as every other person does" (TOB 77:4). This is why he indicates that the call to celibacy is not only a matter of formation but of *transformation* (see TOB 81:5). To the degree that a person lives this transformation he is not bound to indulge his lusts. He is free with the freedom of the gift. For such a person, sacrificing sexual union (the icon) for the sake of the kingdom (the reality to which the icon points) not only becomes a possibility, it becomes quite attractive. The reality is infinitely more attractive than the icon! Those who think otherwise have turned the icon into an idol.

St. Paul's Teaching

In this context it is important to understand properly St. Paul's teaching about marriage and celibacy in 1 Corinthians, chapter seven. He writes that people who "cannot exercise self-control ... should marry. For it is better to marry than to be aflame with passion" (v. 9). Is marriage only intended for those who "can't handle" celibacy? Does marriage suddenly make a person's lack of self-control (lust) "OK"? Not according to John Paul II.

The Pope reminds us that we cannot interpret Paul's words apart from Christ's words about lust. The verb translated "to be aflame" signifies lust. "To marry" signifies the ethical order—the call to overcome lust—that St. Paul consciously introduces in this context (see TOB 101:3). So, according to John Paul II, it seems that St. Paul is saying something like this: "It is better to overcome lust through the grace of marriage than to remain engulfed by its flames."

John Paul II acknowledges that St. Paul's teaching on marriage and celibacy in 1 Corinthians, chapter seven is marked by "his own tone, in some sense, his own 'personal' interpretation" (TOB 82:1). The Pope even asks if St. Paul's statements indicate a "personal aversion" to marriage (see TOB 83:3). When taken out of context, verses such as "It is well for a man not to touch a woman" (v. 1); "I wish that all were [celibate] as I myself am" (v. 7); and "Do not seek marriage" (v. 27) might lead one to believe so. But the Pope demonstrates that a thoughtful reading of the whole text leads to a different conclusion.

St. Paul directly combats the badly mistaken idea circulating in Corinth that marriage and sexual union were sinful. Marriage is a "special gift from God" (v. 7). Spouses "should not refuse one another" in their sexual relationship "except perhaps by agreement" (v. 5). And St. Paul commends those who marry for "doing well" (see v. 38).

Is Celibacy "Better" Than Marriage?

Why, then, does St. Paul say that "he who refrains from marriage will do better" (v. 38)? Based on these words, the Church has traditionally taught that celibacy is an objectively "superior" vocation. But this must be understood with great care lest we fall into serious error. Many have erroneously concluded that if celibacy is "so good," marriage must be "so bad." If refraining from sex makes one "pure and holy," having sex—even in marriage—must make one "tainted and dirty." This is absolutely *not* the mind of the Church! Such devaluations of marriage and sexual union actually stem from the Manichean heresy we spoke of in the first chapter.

John Paul II makes it perfectly clear: "The 'superiority' of [celibacy for the kingdom] to matrimony in the authentic Tradition of the Church never means disparagement of marriage or belittlement of its essential value. It does not ... mean a shift, even implicit, on the Manichean positions, or a support of ways of evaluating or acting based on the Manichean understanding of the body and sexuality." In the authentic teaching of the Church "we do not find any basis whatsoever for the disparagement of marriage" (TOB 77:6).

Celibacy is the "exceptional" calling because marriage remains the "normal" calling in this life. It is "better" not because of celibacy itself, but because it is chosen *for the kingdom*. It is better in the sense that the heavenly marriage (to which celibates devote themselves more directly) is superior to the earthly marriage. Christian celibacy gives those who live it authentically an even more intense "foretaste" of the communion to come with God and with all the saints.

Does this mean if we *really* wanted to follow God we would all be celibates? No. As St. Paul writes, "Each has his own special gift from God, one of one kind and one of another" (v. 7). We must carefully and prayerfully discern which "gift" God has given us. Subjectively speaking, the "better" vocation is the one God calls us to as our own personal gift. If marriage is your gift, rejoice! This is your path to happiness. If celibacy is your gift, rejoice! This is your path to happiness.

Marriage and Celibacy Complement Each Other

Marriage and celibacy obviously differ in important ways. Yet these differences do not conflict. The values of one and the other vocation interpenetrate. In fact, marriage and celibacy "explain or complete each other" (TOB 78:2). Marriage reveals the spousal nature of the celibate vocation just as the celibate vocation reveals the great value of marital union. Let me explain.

How does marital love shed light on the nature of the celibate vocation? John Paul II writes that the fidelity and "total self-donation" lived by spouses provide a model for the fidelity and self-donation required of those who choose the celibate vocation. Both vocations in their own way express marital or spousal love, which entails "the complete gift of self" (see TOB 78:4). Furthermore, the fruit of children in married life helps celibate men and women realize that they are called to a fruitfulness as well—a fruitfulness of the spirit. In these ways we see how the "natural" reality of marriage points us to the "supernatural" reality of celibacy for the kingdom. In fact, full knowledge and appreciation of God's plan for marriage and family life are indispensable for the celibate person. As the Pope expresses it, in order for the celibate person "to be fully *aware of what he is choosing* ... he must also be fully aware *of what he is renouncing*" (TOB 81:2).

Celibacy, in turn, "has a particular importance and particular eloquence for those who live a conjugal life" (TOB 78:2). Celibacy, as a direct anticipation of the marriage to come, shows couples what their union is a sacrament of. In other words, celibacy helps married couples realize that their love also is oriented toward "the kingdom." Furthermore, by abstaining from sexual union, celibates demonstrate the great value of sexual union. How so? A sacrifice only has value to the degree that the thing sacrificed has value. For example, we do not give up sin for Lent; we are supposed to give up sin *all the time*. If our sacrifice is to mean anything, we must sacrifice something of *real value*. The Church values celibacy so highly *precisely* because she values what it sacrifices—sexual union and all that is connected to it—so highly.

Once again, the self-denial involved in such a sacrifice must not be conceived as a repression of sexuality. Celibacy for the kingdom is meant to be a fruitful living out of the redemption of sexual desire, understood as the desire to make of oneself a "sincere gift" for others.

Celibacy Expresses the Spousal Meaning of the Body

As we can see, marriage and celibacy are much more closely related than most people realize. Both vocations provide "a full answer" to the meaning of sexuality (see TOB 85:9). That meaning is "self-donation" in the image of God. As a result, it shouldn't surprise us that whenever a culture devalues sexuality, it inevitably devalues both marriage *and* the celibate vocation. The sexual revolution of the twentieth century has certainly demonstrated this in practice.

The Pope insists that the celibate life Christ spoke of must flow from a deep and mature awareness of the spousal meaning of the body. Only on this basis does celibacy for the kingdom "*find a full guarantee and motivation*" (TOB 80:5). Thus, if someone were to choose this vocation based on a fear or rejection of sex, or because of deep-seated sexual wounds that prevented a healthy married life, it would not correspond to Christ's invitation (see TOB 80:7).

No one can reject the spousal meaning of his body without doing violence to his humanity as a man or woman made in God's image. The spousal meaning of the body is "the fundamental component of human existence in the world" (TOB 15:5). It reveals that the human person is created to be a gift "for" another. Christ's words about celibacy "show accordingly that this '*for*,' which has been present from the beginning at the basis of marriage, *can also stand at the basis of continence 'for' the kingdom of heaven!*" Therefore, "on the basis of the same spousal meaning of [the] body ... there can be formed the love that commits man to marriage for the whole duration of his life, but there can be formed also the love that commits man for his whole life to continence 'for the kingdom of heaven'" (TOB 80:6).

The point is that our sexuality calls us to give ourselves away in life-giving love. The celibate person doesn't reject this call. He just lives it in a different way. Every man, by virtue of the spousal meaning of his body, is called in some way to be both a husband and a father. Every woman, by virtue of the spousal meaning of her body, is called in some way to be both a wife and a mother. As an image of Christ, the celibate man "marries" the Church. Through his bodily gift of self he bears numerous "spiritual children." As an image of the Church, the celibate woman "marries" Christ. Through her bodily gift of self she bears numerous "spiritual children." This is why the terms husband, wife, father, mother, brother, and sister are applicable both to marriage and family life *and* priestly and religious life.

The Celibate Marriage of Joseph and Mary

We will conclude our discussion of celibacy by looking briefly at the "oddity" of the virginal marriage of Mary and Joseph. The Catholic Church teaches that Mary and Joseph were given the exceptional calling to embrace both the celibate vocation and the marital vocation *at the same time.* In other words, they lived the earthly marriage and the heavenly "marriage" simultaneously. In turn, their virginal marriage literally affected the marriage of heaven and earth. For the fruitfulness of their total, virginal gift of self witnessed to and served the Word made flesh—heaven come to earth (see TOB 75:3). In this way Joseph and Mary "became the first witnesses of a fruitfulness different from that of the flesh, that is, the fruitfulness of the Spirit: 'What is begotten in her comes from the Holy Spirit' (Matthew 1:20)" (TOB 75:2).

Joseph and Mary remained virgins not because "sex is bad." As a married couple, they were given the exceptional calling to live their sexuality according to its ultimate meaning—total self-donation to God. By embracing that "heavenly dimension" of sexuality on earth, they enabled heaven to penetrate earth. Recall that sexual union, from the beginning, was meant to foreshadow the union of God and man, Christ and the Church. Undoing Eve's "no," Mary, the new Eve, represents the whole human race in giving her "yes" to God's marriage proposal (see CCC 411, 505). In a sense, even in her journey on earth, Mary was already participating in the "nuptials" of heaven.

If the Church holds out the Holy Family as a model for all families, this does not imply that married couples who want to be "really holy" should never have sex. If such were the case, "holy" families would eventually mean *no* families due to their failure to procreate. Joseph and Mary are a model for all married couples because of their example of total self-donation. The normal call is for spouses to model the Holy Family by living their "one flesh" union in total self-donation. In this way, spouses also "bring Christ to the world" because the marital embrace—when lived as God intends—proclaims the mystery of Christ (see Ephesians 5:31-32).

We will unfold the way in which the "one flesh" union proclaims the mystery of Christ more precisely in Part II.

Part II:

THE SACRAMENT

Chapter 6

MARRIAGE AS A DIVINE GIFT

"God himself is the author of marriage." He
"has judged [it] worthy of special gifts, healing,
perfecting, and exalting gifts of grace."
– GS 48, 49

We continue to seek an answer to the question "How can I live my life in a way that brings true happiness?" The quick answer is to love as God loves, in "sincere self-giving." Celibacy for the kingdom is one way to do this. But it is clearly the exception to the rule. Marriage and family life remain the normal vocation. However, as John Paul II observes, "If someone chooses marriage, he must choose it exactly as it was instituted by the Creator 'from the beginning'" (TOB 79:6). If married life is based on anything other than God's original plan, it is sure to disappoint; it is sure to lead to heartache rather than happiness.

How, then, can couples reclaim God's original plan? The *Catechism* responds: "By coming to restore the original order of creation disturbed by sin, [Christ] himself gives the strength and grace to live marriage in the new dimension of the Reign of God." Therefore, "by following Christ, renouncing themselves, and taking up their crosses ... spouses will be able to 'receive' the original meaning of marriage and live it with the help of Christ" (CCC 1615). As we will see more clearly in this chapter and the next, marriage, as a sacrament, plunges spouses right into the heart of the mystery of Christ.

"The Sacrament"

Marriage, like every other sacrament, has both a divine

73

and a human dimension. Chapters six and seven of this book, in keeping with the Pope's original outline, are divided accordingly. The *divine dimension* refers to the heavenly gift God lavishes on us in the sacrament while the *human dimension* refers to the physical and bodily signs through which God communicates his gift. We see something of both the human and divine dimensions of the sacrament of marriage in Ephesians 5:31-32: "'For this reason a man shall leave his father and mother and be joined to his wife, and the two shall become one flesh.' This is a great mystery, and I mean in reference to Christ and the Church."

Through their union in "one flesh" (the human dimension), spouses are caught up into the "great mystery" of God's covenant love for humanity, Christ's union with the Church (the divine dimension). By calling Part II of his Theology of the Body "The Sacrament," John Paul gives us some insight into the relationship of these two unions (husband-wife and Christ-Church). "The Sacrament" obviously refers to marriage, but it is also broader than that. In the broader sense, it refers to the way in which God's eternal Mystery "has *become visible* and thereby *entered into the sphere of the Sign*" (TOB 95b:6).

In the beginning God's Mystery became visible through the great sign of man and woman's union in marriage. In the "fullness of time" this same Mystery became visible through the far greater sign of Christ's union with the Church (see TOB 97:4). As we will come to understand more deeply in this chapter, the "great mystery" of "the sacrament" is to be found precisely in the fact that these two signs, these two "great sacraments," have become *one*. These two "great signs"—the union of husband–wife and the union of Christ–Church—express *one Mystery* and, thus, form one "great sacrament": *The* Sacrament (see TOB 95b:7). We learn this primarily through the marvelous teaching of St. Paul in Ephesians 5.

A *"Summa" of Christian Teaching*

The whole of St. Paul's text from Ephesians 5:21-32 serves as the basis for the Pope's reflections on the sacrament, but one verse in particular stands out. In fact, it often causes the hair on the back of women's necks to stand up: "Wives, be subject [or submit] to your husbands." Oh boy, here we go ...

It is true that some men throughout history have used this verse to justify their own sinful domination of women. (According to Genesis 3:16, male domination is the direct result of *sin*.) Before you dismiss St. Paul as a male chauvinist, though, wait until you discover John Paul II's winning interpretation of his words. The Pope resurrects the true meaning of Ephesians 5 by applying one of the most important rules of biblical interpretation: read each verse *in context*. Here is the entire passage:

> Be subject to one another out of reverence for Christ. Wives, be subject to your husbands, as to the Lord. For the husband is the head of the wife as Christ is the head of the Church, his body, and is himself its Savior. As the Church is subject to Christ, so let wives also be subject in everything to their husbands. Husbands, love your wives, as Christ loved the Church and gave himself up for her, that he might sanctify her, having cleansed her by the washing of water with the word, that he might present the Church to himself in splendor, without spot or wrinkle or any such thing, that she might be holy and without blemish. Even so husbands should love their wives as their own bodies. He who loves his wife loves himself. For no man ever hates his own flesh, but nourishes and cherishes it, as Christ does the Church, because we are members of his body. "For this reason a man shall leave his father and mother and be joined to his wife, and the two shall become one flesh." This is a great mystery, and I mean in reference to Christ and the Church (Ephesians 5:21-32).

Reaching beyond the polemics we must try "to understand if possible 'to the very depths' what wealth of the truth revealed by God is contained within the scope of [this] stupendous page" (TOB 87:6). This "key and classic text," as the Pope describes it, immerses us in the glory and greatness of God's plan for creating us male and female and calling us to sexual union. Even more, it serves as "the compendium or *summa*, in some sense, *of the teaching about God and man* which was brought to fulfillment by Christ" (LF 19).

If God's spousal love for humanity was only "half-open" in the Old Testament, here the mystery is "fully unveiled (without ceasing to be a mystery, of course)" (TOB 95:7). In turn, through this revelation of God's spousal love, we become witnesses "of a particular encounter of [God's] mystery with the very essence of the vocation to marriage" (TOB 89:7).

St. Paul's Evangelical Genius

Like all of us, St. Paul was certainly affected by his culture. As the Pope writes, he "is not afraid to accept the concepts that were characteristic of the mentality and customs of that time. ... Certainly, our contemporary sensitivity is different ... and the social position of women in comparison with men is different" (TOB 89:5, 6). But if we simply dismiss St. Paul's words as nothing but a product of his "politically incorrect" culture, we miss his evangelical genius altogether. Like any great evangelist, St. Paul appeals to the language and customs of the culture he is trying to reach, while injecting that language and those customs with the mystery of Christ.

In Ephesians 4 (remember *context* is key), St. Paul states explicitly that Christians "must no longer live as the Gentiles do." They "are darkened in their understanding ... due to their hardness of heart." So put off "your old nature which ... is corrupt through deceitful lusts ... and be renewed in the spirit of your minds, and put on the new nature, created after the likeness of God in true righteousness and holiness" (Ephesians 4:17-18, 22-24). This should all sound very familiar to us by now. Who also spoke of "hardness of heart" and how it distorts the sexual relationship? Who also invited men and women to live in "true righteousness and holiness" by experiencing redemption from lust? Like Christ, St. Paul is calling men and women *back to God's original plan!* He is calling men and women to live according to the divine image in which God originally made them.

When the contested (and detested) verses of Ephesians 5 are read in their full context, we realize that—far from demeaning women and absolving abusive men—St. Paul is restoring the only sure foundation for the proper balance of love between the sexes. In effect, we might conclude that St. Paul is saying something like this: "Sure, since this is the language you are used to, we can talk about 'submission' in marriage. But that means one thing to the Gentiles. Here is how it must look for followers of Christ."

Mutual Subjection and Reverence for Christ

Notice that the first thing St. Paul says to spouses is "Be subject [or submit] to *one another* out of reverence for Christ" (v. 21). As John Paul II emphasizes, Ephesians 5 calls spouses to a *mutual* subjection. Those who think St. Paul was simply regurgitating cultural prejudice against women do not understand how counter-cultural this idea was.

The Pope insists that when St. Paul writes "be subject to your husbands" (v. 22), he "does not intend to say that ... marriage is a contract of domination by the husband over the wife ... Love makes the *husband simultaneously subject to the wife*" (TOB 89:3, 4). He adds that being "subject" to one's spouse means being "completely given" (TOB 90:2). Therefore mutual subjection means "a reciprocal gift of self" (see TOB 89:4). It means both spouses realize and live the spousal meaning of their bodies, which calls them to mutual and sincere self-giving.

Christ, who "gave up his body" for his Bride, must be the source and the model of this self-giving. Christian spouses give themselves up for one another "out of reverence for Christ" (v. 21). John Paul II goes so far as to say that this reverence is none other than a *"spiritually mature form*" of the mutual attraction of the sexes, of that "*fascination* of the man for femininity and of the woman for masculinity" (TOB 117b:4). In other words, "reverence for Christ" results from a lived experience of the redemption of sexual attraction and desire. Through ongoing conversion we gradually come to experience that mature level of purity we spoke of previously.

Pure men and women *see* the mystery of Christ revealed through their bodies. It is not just a religious concept; pure men and women *feel* it in their hearts. They realize that the call to union inscribed in their sexuality is a "great mystery" that proclaims the union of Christ and the Church. When we experience this as the "content" of our sexual attractions, we do not want to lust—we want to genuflect. When we live as St. Paul calls us to, lust is *unthinkable*. The "great mystery" of sexuality fills us instead with profound amazement, awe, and wonder. In other words, it fills us with *reverence for Christ.*

The Virtuous Husband

As a practical example of husbands living a redeemed sexuality in subjection to their wives, I often point to this eye-opening passage from the Pope's book *Love and Responsibility*. It not only shows that Karol Wojtyla (John Paul's pre-papal name) was no prude, but, more importantly, it calls men to self-control and tenderness out of deep respect and reverence for their wives. Wojtyla wrote that if a husband is truly to love his wife, "it is necessary to insist that intercourse must not serve merely as a means of allowing [his] climax. ... The man must take [the] difference between male and female reactions into account ... so that climax may be reached [by] both ... and as far as possible occur in both simultaneously." The husband must do this "not for hedonistic, but for altruistic reasons." In this case, if "we take into account the shorter and more violent curve of arousal in the man, [such] tenderness on his part in the context of marital intercourse acquires the significance of an act of virtue" (LR, pp. 272, 275).

Please read this passage to anyone and everyone who thinks the Church is "down on sex." How far from the truth! As an astonished engaged woman once exclaimed when I read this passage, "*The Pope rocks!*"

History attests that few men express the tenderness and virtue that John Paul spoke of in the passage above. As a whole, women have suffered greatly at the hands of male lust and domination, just as Genesis predicted (see Genesis 3:16). So, to all the women reading this book, if you have never heard this, it is long overdue. Allow me, as a representative of the male side of the human race, to apologize humbly for the way male lust has wounded you. The wounds go so very deep in a woman's soul, and I am so very, very sorry. Please forgive us. We know not what we do.

To the men I say, get ready. Are you up to the mission St. Paul assigns us? I am going to call you forth into battle—a battle that involves all the courage and stamina you can muster; a battle that involves much sacrifice. We must be men who are willing to sacrifice rather than ever indulge our lusts.

Submission within the Spousal Analogy

In a world void of such heroic, sacrificial men, the feminist revolt against Ephesians 5 is quite understandable. In the absence of redemption, St. Paul's words can only be viewed as an admonition for wives to resign themselves to male lust and tyranny. But redemption has been accomplished! The knowledge that Christ died and rose again to empower us to live according to God's original plan of love deeply imbues St. Paul's entire teaching on marriage. He presents redemption itself through the analogy of spousal love and sexual union.

According to the analogy, the wife images the Church and the husband images Christ. The analogy obviously breaks down (e.g., no husband perfectly images Christ), yet it speaks volumes not only about Christ's "spousal" love for us, but also about the very essence and meaning of marriage. We learn that "marriage corresponds to the vocation of Christians only when it mirrors the love that Christ, the Bridegroom, gives to the Church, his Bride, and which the Church ... seeks to give back to Christ" (TOB 90:2). Apart from this model, marriage can sink quite quickly into a form of oppression, especially for women.

Again, St. Paul uses the language of his day but injects it with an entirely new, redemptive meaning. When we understand the nature of the analogy he is using, it makes sense for him to say, "Wives be subject [or submit] to your husbands as to the Lord" (v. 22). One way I explain "submission" in this context is, "Wives, put yourself *under* (sub) the *mission* of your husband." What is the mission of the husband? Here it is gentlemen: "Husbands, love your wives *as Christ loved the Church.*" How did Christ love the Church? He "gave himself up for her" (v. 25)—unto death! Christ said that he came not to be served *but to serve*, and to lay down his life for his Bride (see Matthew 20:28).

"Headship" Is a Call to Serve

Why are we so quick to accuse St. Paul of justifying male domination? Based on what we have unfolded, when St. Paul writes, "Wives, submit to your husbands" he is saying, "Wives, allow your husbands to *serve you.*" To which I respond, "Who has got it worse here?" We have got the whole thing flipped upside down! Not that the wife is the master and the husband a slave. Power, control, domination—these are the wrong paradigms altogether, regardless of who is "the boss." Christian marriage calls spouses to a *mutual service*, or, as St. Paul says, a mutual "subjection." Yet, according to the nature of sexual difference, each lives this service in different, complementary ways.

If Ephesians says that "the husband is the head of the wife as Christ is the head of the Church," this means the husband must be *the first to serve* (see Luke 22:25-26). There is a "sacred order" to love. In imaging Christ and the Church, John Paul II writes that "the husband is above all *he who loves,* and the wife, on the other hand is *she who is loved.*" Thus, we can conclude with the Pope that "the wife's 'submission' to the husband ... means above all 'the experiencing of love.' This is all the more so, because this 'submission' refers to the image of the submission of the Church to Christ, which certainly consists in experiencing his love" (TOB 92:6).

Is this demeaning towards women? Imagine what marriage would be like if husbands took St. Paul's words to heart. Imagine if husbands throughout the world preferred to die rather than ever violate the dignity of their wives. Is not this the example Christ gave us? And is not this the kind of love women are looking for? Is not this what the knight-in-shining-armor romantic fantasy is all about?

Restoration of Holiness

Spouses who commit themselves to St. Paul's vision of marriage—properly understood—find that the grace of their sacrament (in conjunction with the other sacraments) gradually re-inflates their "tires." In other words, they experience their love for each other as something beautifully healing and redemptive. Marital love not only participates in the mystery of creation through pro-creation, it also participates in the mystery of redemption. As the Pope says, authentic marital love is "redeeming, saving love, the love with which man has been loved by God from eternity in Christ" (TOB 90:2). Here we see very clearly the divine dimension of the sacrament, the divine gift (grace) communicated through marriage.

Even here on earth, the grace of Christ's spousal love begins restoring in us something of the holiness experienced by the first married couple. "Christ loved the Church and gave himself up for her ... that she might be holy" (vv. 25-27). But, as we all know, holiness is not something automatic. In all our trials and struggles, we must continually open ourselves like a bride to receive the gift of Christ's love, allowing it to *in*form and *trans*form us. As John Paul II writes, "Holiness is measured according to the 'great mystery' in which the Bride responds with the gift of love to the gift of the Bridegroom" (MD 27).

Holiness, then, is not first a matter of *doing*, but of *letting it be done to us* (see Luke 1:38). We must allow Christ to "crucify" all our disordered ways of relating. We must allow him to sanctify us (make us holy) "by the washing of water with the word" (v. 26). Scripture scholars see in this a reference to baptism. It was customary in St. Paul's day for the bride to precede her wedding with a cleansing bath in preparation for her bridegroom. The *Catechism* describes baptism as "the nuptial bath which precedes the wedding feast, the Eucharist" (CCC 1617). St. Paul also alludes to the nuptial gift of the Eucharist when he speaks of the "nourishment" Christ offers his Bride (see v. 29).

But marriage not only sheds light on baptism and the Eucharist. John Paul II observes that marriage serves as the model or *prototype* in some sense of all the sacraments of the new covenant (see TOB 98:2). All the sacraments have a "spousal" character since their purpose is to unite the Bride (the Church) with her Bridegroom (Christ). Through this grand analogy, the union of spouses becomes perhaps the most insightful way of understanding Christianity itself. "The entire Christian life bears the mark of the spousal love of Christ and the Church" (CCC 1617).

Chosen in Christ from the Beginning

Just as God organically inscribed the marital union of Adam and Eve in the mystery of creation, he organically inscribes the "marital" union of the new Adam and the new Eve (Christ and the Church) in the mystery of redemption. Spousal union, in fact, becomes the foundation upon which God constructs the entire mystery of our redemption in Christ (see TOB 95:7). The mystery of redemption "clothes itself, so to speak, in the figure and form of the primordial sacrament [marriage]. To the marriage of the first husband and wife ... corresponds the marriage, or rather the analogy of marriage, of Christ with the Church" (TOB 97:2).

Here, in the "spousal" character of both creation and redemption, we recognize an essential continuity regarding God's plan for humanity. We tend to think of Christ's coming as "plan B," necessitated when man and woman's sin supposedly thwarted "plan A." Our need of redemption from sin certainly flows from the reality of our fall. Yet God's plan for us to share in his own eternal "exchange of love" remains the same yesterday, today, and forever. Sin, you might say, caused a detour in the fulfillment of that plan, but it did not thwart it. God's plan for man continues despite sin. That plan—forever and for always—is that all things would be taken up and united in Christ (see Ephesians 1:10).

John Paul II cannot stress enough that Christ—the Incarnate Christ—has always been at the center of God's plan for man and for the universe. As he wrote in the first line of his first encyclical letter, "Jesus Christ is the center of the universe and of history" (RH 1). God destined us for union with Christ not only after sin and not only to redeem us from sin. God "chose us in [Christ] before the foundation of the world" (Ephesians 1:4).

This means that the grace of original innocence (recall the experiences of original solitude, unity, and nakedness) "was granted in consideration of him [Christ] ... although—according to the dimensions of time and history—it preceded the Incarnation" (TOB 96:5). In other words, the love (grace) man and woman knew "in the beginning" through their bodies was a foretaste or preview in some sense of the love (grace) that Christ would pour out within history through his body. In fact, the love the first couple knew in their bodies *depended* in some sense on the love that Christ would pour out on his Bride, the Church. Creation foreshadows and prepares us for redemption; the union of the first Adam and Eve foreshadows and prepares us for the union of the new Adam and Eve, Christ and the Church.

Again, although it often demands a rethinking of commonly held perceptions, the Incarnation is not an afterthought in God's mind. As the *Catechism* confirms, "From the beginning, God envisaged the glory of the new creation in Christ" (CCC 280). We can conclude this because St. Paul links the "one flesh" union of Genesis with the union of Christ and the Church. "'For this reason a man shall leave his father and mother and be joined to his wife, and the two shall become one flesh.' This is a great mystery, and I mean in reference to Christ and the church" (Ephesians 5:31-32). Right from the beginning— before sin—conjugal union foreshadowed the Incarnation, Christ's union with humanity in "one flesh."

This Is a "Great Mystery"

St. Paul's linking of the "one flesh" union with the union of Christ and the Church "is the most important point of the whole text, *in some sense its keystone*" (TOB 93:1). Both "the union of Christ with the Church and the spousal union of man and woman in marriage are in this way illuminated by a particular supernatural light" (TOB 91:8).

Guided by this supernatural light, St. Paul demonstrates a keen understanding of the "sacramentality" of the body. Recall the broader sense of this term. The body is a "sacrament" in the sense that it makes visible the invisible. In examining Ephesians 5 the Pope recalls his thesis: "The body, in fact, and only the body, is capable of making visible what is invisible: the spiritual and divine. It has been created to transfer into the visible reality of the world the mystery hidden from eternity in God, and thus to be a sign of it" (TOB 96:6; 19:4).

Recall what we mean by "the mystery hidden from eternity in God": (1) *God is a Communion of love* and (2) We are *destined to share in that exchange* through our union with Christ. John Paul writes that the "sacrament consists in *'manifesting'* that *mystery in a sign* that serves not only to proclaim the mystery but also *to accomplish it* in man" (TOB 93:5). Sacramental signs truly bring about what they signify. St. Paul speaks of two signs—one from the order of creation and the other from the order of redemption—that truly communicate God's mystery of love.

In creation, the Pope says that God's mystery of love "became a *visible reality through the union* of the first man and woman" (see Genesis 2:24). In redemption, that same mystery of divine love becomes "*a visible reality in the indissoluble union of Christ with the Church*, which the author of Ephesians presents as the spousal union" (TOB 97:4). With regard to these signs, these two unions, we are speaking "in reference to the entire work of creation and redemption" (TOB 97:5). This is the stupendous capacity of sacramental signs. They mysteriously "contain" ultimate reality and put us in touch with it. They "embrace the universe," as John Paul II says.

The Meaning of Human Life

John Paul II remarks that it is a "particular merit" of St. Paul "that he brought these two signs together [spousal union and the union of Christ and the Church], making of them *the single great sign*, that is, *a great sacrament* (TOB 95b:7). Through this "great sacrament" the "great mystery" of human life is revealed.

The Pope observes that the linking of these two unions is obviously important "to the Christian vocation of husbands and wives." However, it "is equally essential and valid *for the [understanding] of man* in general: for the fundamental problem of understanding him and for the self-understanding of his being in the world." Indeed, it is in this link that we "find the answer to the question about the meaning of 'being a body'" (TOB 102:5).

What is that meaning? We are called to love as Christ loves. This is the new commandment Christ gives us, "Love one another as I have loved you" (John 15:12). How did Christ love us? "This is my body ... *given for you*" (Luke 22:19).

Remember the story of my father-in-law, the tears he shed when he received the Eucharist for the first time after consummating his marriage? My father-in-law realized that day that the meaning of life, the meaning of the universe, is inscribed not only in our souls, but in our bodies: in the "great mystery" of sexual difference and our call to become "one flesh." As we will see even more clearly in the next chapter, spousal union is the "great sign" God has given the world to reveal the mystery of his own love.

Chapter 7

MARRIAGE AS A HUMAN SIGN
OF GOD'S LOVE

"Authentic married love is caught up into divine love."
–GS 48

In chapter six we looked primarily at the mystery of God's eternal love in which marriage participates. This is the *divine dimension* of the sacrament. Now we will look more closely at the *human dimension* of the sacrament—the physical, bodily sign through which God communicates his love in marriage.

We have already said much about the nature of marital love as a "sign" of God's love. But now the Pope gets even more specific. He does so first by developing the concept of the "language of the body" and the need to speak this language truthfully. Then he looks to the lovers in the Song of Songs and to the marriage of Tobias and Sarah as biblical examples of couples who, each in their own way, speak the language of the body truthfully. As John Paul II says, both couples "find their place in what constitutes the sacramental sign of marriage. Both share in the formation of this sign" (TOB 116:5).

The Sacramental Sign of Marriage

Every sacrament has a specific physical sign that communicates the spiritual reality of grace it signifies. For example, the physical sign of baptism—the immersion or infusion of a person with water, together with the invocation of the Trinitarian formula—really and truly communicates a spiritual cleansing of the person's soul from original sin.

What, then, is the sign of the sacrament of marriage that communicates the grace of God's love to the couple?

Simplifying a rather complex discussion, one can recognize that over the centuries there have been two schools of thought about what causes marriage. Most theologians have considered the exchange of vows (marital consent) to be the efficacious cause of marriage. Others have taught that the consummation of marriage in sexual intercourse is the cause. The two views were resolved by Church law centuries ago in this way: Consent is the efficacious cause of marriage. However, consummation of a ratified marriage (between a baptized man and a baptized woman) makes the marriage both intrinsically and extrinsically indissoluble. This is the teaching of John Paul II.

In turn, he observes that the sacramental sign of marriage is one of "manifold contents" (see TOB 105:6). It begins with the exchange of consent, is consummated in sexual intercourse, and is borne in the spouses themselves throughout the whole of their married lives. What makes the husband and wife themselves a sacramental sign of God's spiritual and divine love? Matrimonial consent expressed in and through the body.

Do you remember the Pope's thesis statement? "The body, in fact, and only the body, is capable of making visible what is invisible: the spiritual and divine. It has been created to transfer into the visible reality of the world the mystery hidden from eternity in God, and thus to be a sign of it" (TOB 19:4). Only in this context can we understand marriage as a sacramental sign. Hence, if wedding vows express a "language of the heart"—a "language of the *spirit*"—there must be a corresponding "language of the *body*."

The Language of the Body

We all know that we can speak without uttering a word through the language of our bodies. A wave of the hand says "hello" or "goodbye." A shrug of the shoulders says, "I don't know." A raised fist expresses anger.

What is sexual intercourse meant to express? What is its true language, its true meaning? According to John Paul II, the bodily union of a man and a woman is meant to express divine love. This is what we are called to and this is what we long for. Nothing less ever satisfies our deepest ache. We know that in our hearts.

Precisely here, in the consummation of their sacrament, the spouses are meant to participate in the fullest way in the "great mystery" of divine love, of Christ's union with the Church (see Ephesians 5:31-32). Whether they realize it or not, this is the sacramental power of the "language of their bodies." As the Pope candidly expresses, "Through gestures and reactions, through the whole ...dynamism of tension and enjoyment—whose direct source is the body in its masculinity and femininity, the body in its action and interaction—through all this *man, the person,* 'speaks' ... Precisely on the level of this 'language of the body' ... man and woman reciprocally express *themselves* in the fullest and most profound way made possible for them by ... their masculinity and femininity" (TOB 123:4).

But if "bodily love" is meant to express "the language of 'agape'" (TOB 92:7), we must properly understand this language. Christ's love seems distinguishable by four particular qualities. First, Christ gives his body *freely* ("No one takes my life from me, I lay it down of my own accord," John 10:18). Second, he gives his body *totally*—without reservation, condition, or selfish calculation ("He loved them to the last," John 13:1). Third, he gives his body *faithfully* ("I am with you always," Matthew 28:20). And fourth, he gives his body *fruitfully* ("I came that they may have life," John 10:10). If men and women are to avoid the pitfalls of counterfeit love, and live their vocation to its full, their union must express the same *free, total, faithful, fruitful* love that Christ's body expresses.

Another name for this kind of love is *marriage.* This is precisely what a bride and groom commit to at the altar. The priest or deacon asks them: "Have you come here *freely* and *without reservation* to give yourselves to each other in marriage? Do you promise to be *faithful* until death? Do you promise to *receive children* lovingly from God?" The bride and groom each say "yes."

In turn, spouses are meant to express this same "yes" *with their bodies* whenever they become one flesh. "In fact, the words themselves, 'I take you as my wife/as my husband,'" the Pope says, "can only be fulfilled by conjugal intercourse" (TOB 103:2). With conjugal intercourse "we pass *to the reality* that corresponds to these words. Both the one and the other element are important *with regard to the structure of the sacramental sign*" (TOB 103:3). Intercourse, then, is where the words of the wedding vows *become flesh*. It is where men and women are meant to *incarnate* divine love. It is a fine thing when a couple returns to the Church to renew their vows on a special anniversary, but this should not undermine the fact that every time a husband and wife have intercourse they are meant to renew their wedding vows with the "language of their bodies."

Distinguishing True and False Prophets

The Church's sexual ethic begins to make sense when viewed through this lens. The Church's teaching is not a prudish list of prohibitions. It is a call to embrace our own "greatness," our own God-given dignity. It is a call to live the love we are created for, the love we so ardently desire.

John Paul II goes so far as to describe the body and sexual union as "prophetic." A prophet is someone who speaks for God, who proclaims his mystery. This is what the marital embrace is meant to proclaim. But, as the Pope adds, we must be careful to distinguish true and false prophets (see TOB 106:4). If we can speak the truth with our bodies, we can also speak lies.

We all know it is possible to lie with our bodies. Suppose a used-car salesman knowingly sells you a lemon and then shakes your hand. Didn't he just lie with his body? What about the kiss of Judas? It was a lie. And who do you think prompts us to lie with our bodies? Could it be ... *Satan*!? *Saturday Night Live* "Church Lady" humor aside, the "father of lies" wants us to speak his own language with our bodies.

Why? To keep us from the "great mystery" of Christ's union with the Church—that is, to keep us from eternal life.

Recall from chapter one that the battle for man's soul is fought over the truth of his body. If the body is meant to sing the greatest of all songs—the Song of Songs—we must be well aware that there is an enemy who hates the divine-human harmony of this song and is literally hell-bent on inserting his own sour notes. If God designed the body to be a sign of his own love and life, the enemy wants to counter that sign with lust and death. As John Paul observed, "[When spouses] unite as husband and wife, they ... find themselves in the situation in which *the powers of good and evil fight against each other.*" Their choices and acts, in fact, "take on the whole weight of human existence in the union of the two" (TOB 115:2,3).

How, then, in the midst of such a sobering battle, can men and women be sure that love and life will win? John Paul turns to the lovers of the Song of Songs and the marriage of Tobias and Sarah as two shining examples of the triumph of love and life over lust and death.

The Biblical Ode to Erotic Love

Why is the Song of Songs the favorite biblical book of the mystics? Why have the saints written more commentaries on the Song of Songs than on any other book in the Bible? Because the erotic poetry of the Song provides a language —certainly inadequate, but in the experience of many of the greatest saints, the *least* inadequate—for expressing the burning passion of God's love and the experience of union to which all are called with God. God's eternal plan, let us recall, is to "marry" us—to live with us in an eternal union of love that the Bible compares to the union of spouses in "one flesh."

Yet the Song of Songs is not merely an allegory of God's "spiritual" love. John Paul II observes that a growing number of biblical scholars maintain that the Song of Songs is "to be taken simply as what it manifestly is: a song of human love" (TOB 108: note 95). For "human love, created and blessed by God, can be the theme of an inspired biblical book" (TOB 108: note 97).

John Paul seems to agree with the view of one scholar who writes that those who have "forgotten the lovers" or "petrified them into pretense" have not interpreted the Song correctly. "'He who does not believe in the human love of the spouses, he who must ask forgiveness for the body, does not have the right to rise higher ... With the affirmation of human love, by contrast, it is possible to discover the revelation of God in it'" (TOB 108: note 96).

This confirms an essential element of incarnational/ sacramental reality. Grace—the mystery of God's life and covenant love—is communicated *through* the "stuff" of our humanity, not despite it. The "content of the Song of Songs is at the same time sexual and sacred." When we ignore the sacred, we see the Song merely as a secular erotic poem. But when we ignore the sexual, we fall into *allegorism*—that is, we ignore the physical and sensual reality of the lovers. "It is only by putting these two aspects together that one can read the book in the right way" (TOB 108: note 97).

Recall that our goal in this chapter is to reflect on the human dimension of marriage as a physical sign of God's life and love. This is precisely what the erotic poetry of the Song of Songs helps us to do.

The Bride as "Sister"

Interestingly, the lover in the Song repeatedly refers to his beloved as "sister" *before* calling her "bride." "You have ravished my heart, my sister, my bride, you have ravished my heart with one glance of your eyes ... How sweet is your love, my sister, my bride!" (4:9-10). These words are "impregnated," the Pope says, "with a particular content" (TOB 110:1). It is as if the lovers in the Song had "descended from the same family circle, as though from infancy they had been united by memories of the common hearth. In this way, they reciprocally feel as close as brother and sister who owe their existence to the same mother" (TOB 110:1).

John Paul observes that "through marriage man and

woman become brother and sister in a special way" (TOB 114:3). Authentic marital love always recognizes one's spouse as a brother or sister that shares the same humanity. Both male and female are made in the image and likeness of God. In this way, recognizing his beloved first as "sister" echoes Adam's words, "This at last is bone of my bones and flesh of my flesh" (Genesis 2:23).

While the idea of being recognized first as a "sister" usually brings great relief to the woman, John Paul observes that it presents a certain *challenge* for the man (see TOB 109:4). More specifically, it challenges him to assess his motives. Is he motivated by love or by lust, by the sincere gift of self or merely by a desire to gratify himself? The normal man recoils at the idea of lusting after his sister—*and so should a man recoil at the thought of lusting after his bride!* This is precisely the point. The lover of the Song accepts this challenge and does not hesitate to call his beloved "my sister." With such a recognition, he demonstrates that his desire for her as "bride" is not one of lust but of love. With *"a disinterested tenderness"* (TOB 110:2) the lover desires only to be a sincere gift to his beloved according to the image of God.

Garden Closed, Fountain Sealed

The groom demonstrates the genuine character of his love all the more when he says, "A garden locked is my sister, my bride, a garden closed, a fountain sealed" (4:12). The Pope observes that these metaphors remain in a very strict relation with the union of the sexes and, thus, help us to understand its mystery, especially the mystery of "the woman" (see TOB 110:7). We can see the great value of these expressions, John Paul says, in their ability to convey the profoundly personal dimension and meaning of the union of the lovers. "The language of metaphors—poetic language—seems to be especially appropriate and precise in this sphere" (TOB 110:8).

Both of these metaphors—"garden closed" and "fountain sealed"—express the whole *personal dignity of the female sex.* They speak with profound reverence of the mystery of the feminine body and—since the body expresses the person—of the feminine personality. These expressions indicate, as John Paul II poignantly observes, that the "bride *presents herself to the eyes of the man as the master of her own mystery*" (TOB 110:7). The groom must —and in the Song of Songs does—respect the fact that he cannot "master" his bride: he cannot, must not, dominate or control her. She is in control of her own person, her own "mystery." For every human person is an inviolable mystery as a unique reflection of God's own Mystery.

The point is that authentic love affords a certain "entering" into the mystery of the other person *without ever violating the mystery of the person* (see TOB 111:1). If a person's "love" violates the one loved, then *it is not love* and should not be called love. It is love's counterfeit—lust. If the lover is to enter this "garden" and participate in the woman's mystery, he cannot barge in or break down the door. Nor can he manipulate her into surrendering the key. This would be rape. If he is to respect woman as "master of her own mystery," all the lover can do is entrust himself to her freedom. All he can do is "knock at the door" and respectfully await her response.

The lover in the Song initiates the gift, making his desire clear: "Open to me, my sister, my love, my dove, my perfect one; for my head is wet with dew" (5:2). And she hears him: "Listen, my beloved is knocking" (5:2). But he puts "his hand to the latch" (5:4) only with her freely given "yes"—a yes given without any hint of being coerced or manipulated. In total freedom, she surrenders to him; she opens her garden to him, making it *his*: "Awake, O north wind, and come, O south wind! Blow upon my garden, let its fragrance be wafted abroad. Let my beloved come to his garden, and eat its choicest fruits" (4:16).

Thus, in the course of their dialogue of love, "*the 'garden closed' opens up in some way before the eyes of the bridegroom's soul and body*" (TOB 111:4). And with profound reverence and awe ("Submit to one another *out of reverence* ...") he beholds her mystery unveiled. He comes to her delighting in her gift, remaining ever in awe of her freely opened garden: "I come to my garden, my sister, my bride, I gather my myrrh with my spice, I eat my honeycomb with my honey, I drink my wine with my milk" (5:1).

These boldly erotic verses of this Song of Songs reveal the mystery of "authentic love" (TOB 110:9). The spouses' ecstatic love provides an "essential sign of holiness" (TOB 109:2). In other words, the spouses in the Song are correctly "reading" the true "language of their bodies" as a sign of divine love. Thus, the human dimension of their sacrament (their human love and sexual union) truly communicates the divine dimension (God's love and grace).

Set Me as a Seal

Consummation is the specific moment in which a ratified marriage becomes intrinsically and extrinsically indissoluble. In this way "the man and the woman together ... constitute the sign of the reciprocal gift of self, which *sets the seal on their whole life*" (TOB 111:5). This is the *power* and *meaning* of sexual union as God designed it. Sexual intercourse has a "language" that proclaims: "I am totally yours unto death. I belong to you and you to me until death do us part."

It is not just that sexual union belongs "in" marriage. Rather, it is that sexual union—as God designed it—has an inherently *marital* meaning. That is why sexual intercourse is called the *marital* embrace. Sex is only what it is meant to be when it expresses a love that is "strong as death." The bride confirms her knowledge of this when she says, "Set me as a seal upon your heart ... for love is strong as death ... Its flashes are flashes of fire, a most vehement flame. Many waters cannot quench love, neither can floods drown it" (8:6-7).

John Paul says that these words bring us to "the peak" of the Song's declaration of love. They seem to present the final chords of the Song, the "final chords in the 'language of the body'." When we read that "love is strong as death" we discover "the closure and crowning of everything in the Song of Songs that begins with the metaphor 'garden closed' and 'fountain sealed'" (TOB 111:6).

With these words, the lover had presented himself to his beloved not as one superficially attracted to her body. Rather, he presented himself as one who was captivated and fascinated by her entire mystery as a woman, as one ready to uphold the whole personal dignity of her sexuality, as one desirous of honoring her as a feminine person, as a sister and a bride—unto death. Here we see that a woman can only open her sacred "garden" to her lover and remain inviolate if she is assured that he is ready and willing to commit his *entire life* to her, if she is assured that he has set her *as a seal upon his heart*, if she is assured that his love will be *strong as death*. The love that is strong as death is called "marriage."

Do you remember that 1960s song by the Shirelles, "Will You Still Love Me Tomorrow"? Listen to these poignant lyrics:

> *Is this a lasting treasure?*
> *Or just a moment's pleasure?*
> *Can I believe the magic of your sighs?*
> *Will you still love me tomorrow?*

Oh, the *ache* in the feminine heart! If any woman reading this book ever finds herself wondering the same thing when a man is putting the moves on her, here is the song you should be singing: "Stop, in the name of love ... before you break my heart!" And every man reading this book should "think it o-o-ver..."

The Church does not impose on us the idea that love should be permanent. Permanence is what the heart longs for. In her teaching that sex is meant to express permanent love (that is, marital love), the Church is simply inviting us to be true to the "song" that wells up from the deepest recesses of our souls. Listen to it! It is the *Song of Songs*.

Sexual Union Is a Test of Life-or-Death

If the lovers in the Song of Songs help us distinguish between authentic love and lust, the marriage of Tobias and Sarah in the Book of Tobit demonstrates just what is at stake in this distinction. From the first moment of their marriage, Tobias and Sarah had *to face the test of life-or-death.* "The words about love 'strong as death,' spoken by the spouses of the Song of Songs ... here take on the character of a real test" (TOB 114:6).

As this Old Testament story goes, Sarah had already been married seven times, but, because of the work of a demon, each groom *died* before having intercourse with her (see Tobit 6:13-14). (Talk about an anti-climactic honeymoon—and seven times in a row!) Then an angel appears to Tobias and tells him that *he* is to marry Sarah. John Paul II—man of keen observation that he is—remarks that Tobias had reason to be afraid. In fact, on the day of their wedding, Sarah's father was already digging Tobias's grave! (see Tobit 8:9)

Tobias courageously faces the test. He takes Sarah as his wife, consummates the marriage—and lives. Why does he live? Because "during the test of the first wedding night, *love supported by prayer is revealed as stronger than death*" (TOB, p. 597). Love "is victorious because it prays" (TOB, p. 601). Take a careful look at Tobias and Sarah's prayer. It contains a short review of everything we have discussed in the Pope's Theology of the Body.

> "Blessed are you, O God ... and blessed be your holy and glorious name for ever .... You made Adam and gave him Eve his wife as a helper and support. You said, 'It is not good that the man should be alone; let us make a helper for him like himself.' And now, O Lord, I am not taking this sister of mine because of lust, but with sincerity. Grant that I may find mercy and grow old together with her." And she said with him, "Amen" (Tobit 8:5-8).

John Paul describes this prayer as the spouses' "conjugal creed" (see TOB 116:2). This creed originates from the depth of *love* in the new spouses' hearts and expresses itself in the *life*-giving language of their bodies. As such, this "creed" serves as a precise antidote to the demon's plot to write *lust* into their hearts and *death* into their bodies.

Tobias first praises God for his sheer goodness. Then, as Christ will direct us to do, he sets his heart on God's original plan for marriage. He calls Sarah "sister" like the lover in the Song of Songs. He contrasts lust with the sincere gift of self. He knows that he needs God's mercy to live the truth of love, and he longs to spend his whole life with her. Sarah's "Amen" demonstrates that she shares one and the same desire.

Tobias' love for Sarah is a "type" of Christ's love for the Church. Christ stared death in the face on the "marriage bed" of the Cross, thus consummating his love for the Church and conquering death by rising to new life. Tobias' also stared death in the face on his marriage bed, and inspired with sacrificial (Christ-like) love, he also conquered death. After seven men had succumbed, Tobias *consummates the marriage and lives!*

If sexual union is a "test of life-or-death," then in the face of authentic spousal love, death has no chance. "Where, O death, is your victory? Where, O death, is your sting?" (1 Corinthians 15:55). Spouses who by God's grace love one another according to God's original plan— and who trust in God's mercy when they fail to love one another rightly—have no fear of this "test." They are ready and willing to place themselves "between the forces of good and evil ... because love is confident in the victory of good and is ready to do everything in order that good may conquer" (TOB 115:2).

Spousal Love as Prayer

We have already learned much about the "great mystery" of Ephesians 5. At the end of his chapter on marriage as a human sign of divine love, John Paul returns to this classic text to reconfirm even more deeply the profound meaning of joining in "one flesh." He observes that if the sacramental sign of marriage is based on the "language of the body" reread in the truth of love, then Ephesians 5 offers us the "*definitive*" expression of this sign reread in the truth of love.

The Song of Songs contains "the language of the body' in all the richness of its subjective meaning" (TOB 117:2). In other words, the lover's duet in the Song allows us in some way to enter their interior, subjective experience of love, as does the story of Tobias and Sarah. Ephesians 5, on the other hand, "contains *the 'objective' confirmation of this language* in its entirety" (TOB 117:2). There we read that the "one flesh" union is a "great mystery" that is meant to express and proclaim the love of Christ and the Church. Despite what a given couple might express subjectively, Ephesians 5 presents the objective truth of the language of the body.

The internal goal (and life-long challenge!) of every marriage is for the spouses to ensure that what they express *subjectively* in their sexual union confirms the *objective* truth of God's plan. As countless couples can attest, simply getting married is not enough to make sexual union something holy and beautiful. Marriage is the objective prerequisite to experience the true glory and holiness of sex. But the couple's *ethos*—their inner orientation and desires—must correspond to the true dignity of the person and the true meaning of spousal love. This, of course, calls for life-long conversion and healing. In a word, it demands a life of deep *prayer*.

Prayer, as the *Catechism* teaches, is where we "let our masks fall and turn our hearts back to the Lord who loves us, so as to hand ourselves over to him as an offering to be purified and transformed" (CCC 2711). This is precisely what Tobias and Sarah did before uniting—from within the bridal chamber, they sought the Lord in prayer: "And now, O Lord, I am not taking this sister of mine because of lust, but with sincerity. Grant that I may find mercy ... And Sarah said with him, 'Amen'" (Tobit 8:7–8). Here we witness *"the moment of purification"* to which spouses must submit themselves if they wish to express the spousal meaning of the body in all its truth (see TOB 116:3).

To the degree that this profound integration between objective reality and subjective experience occurs, John Paul says that spouses experience the language of the body for what it is. They experience it as *the language of the Church's liturgy* (see TOB 116:5). This idea brings us to the pinnacle of the value John Paul places on spousal love. Here we cross the threshold of the "great mystery" and enter into the most profound integration of the sexual and the sacred.

In the *Catechism* we learn that in the Christian tradition, liturgy "means the participation of the People of God in 'the work of God'" (CCC 1069). The work of God refers above all to the "great mystery" of our redemption in Christ accomplished through his death and resurrection. To say that spousal love is "liturgical" is to say that it participates in this "great mystery." Liturgy is also the Church's "celebration of divine worship" (CCC 1070). When lived according to the "great mystery" of God's designs, the marital embrace itself becomes a profound prayer. It becomes "eucharistic" —an act of thanksgiving offered to God for the joyous gift of sharing in his life and love (the word *eucharist* means "thanksgiving"). According to the analogy, we might even view the marital bed as an altar upon which spouses offer their bodies in living sacrifice, holy and acceptable to God. This is their spiritual act of worship (see Romans 12:1).

The Ineffable Joy of Nuptial Union

Such a lofty vision of marital intercourse may seem hopelessly unrealistic, even undesirable to some: *"Come on, sex is meant to be a prayer? Like my husband would ever go for that!"* Or, *"Who wants sex to be prayerful? What a turn-off!"*

While it may be the case that a given spouse has no interest in pursuing a "prayerful sex life," the above sentiments reflect tragically misinformed notions of both sex and prayer. Yes, authentic prayer not only *can* but *should* "turn off" lust. But authentic prayer *can* and certainly *should* "turn on" the noble and deep flowing passion of genuine sexual love. In fact, the great mystical tradition of the Church describes prayer itself with the language of the analogy of erotic love. Prayer, from this perspective, is the opening of the bride to the gift of the Bridegroom and the impregnation of the bride with divine life.

As John Paul II expressed it, prayer is a "dialogue of love" that "can progress ... to the point of rendering the person wholly possessed by the divine Beloved." Such divine intimacy in prayer "demands an intense spiritual commitment and is no stranger to painful purifications (the 'dark night'). But it leads, in various possible ways, to the ineffable joy experienced by the mystics as 'nuptial union'" (NMI, n. 33). Here, just to clarify, the Pope means nuptial union ... *with God.*

What we are learning in the Theology of the Body is that only to the degree that we are living in "nuptial union" with God are we capable of living in authentic "nuptial union" with others. This is what joining in "one flesh" is: a sacramental sign of union with God. Could there possibly be a more exalted notion of sexual union than to see it as a sign of union with God?

Imaging God's Love

If the lovers of the Song of Songs proclaim the joy of living the true sign of marital love while Tobias and Sarah face a test of life-or-death to reclaim the truth of that sign, what light does this shed on the Church's teaching on sexual morality?

Ultimately, all questions of sexual morality come down to one very simple question: Does this act truly image God's *free, total, faithful, fruitful* love or doesn't it? If it doesn't, it is a lesser love, a counterfeit that can never satisfy. Think of it this way: if sexual intercourse is meant to be a renewal of wedding vows, how healthy would a marriage be if spouses were regularly unfaithful to their vows? On the other hand, how healthy would a marriage be if spouses regularly renewed their vows, expressing an ever-increasing commitment to them? As we will see more clearly in the next chapter, this is precisely what is at stake in the Church's teaching on sexual morality.

But it is not up to us to "try real hard" to love as God loves. *We simply cannot do it.* Our job, rather, is to open to the gift of his love that he wants to pour into our hearts.

"God's love has been poured into our hearts through the Holy Spirit who has been given to us" (Romans 5:5). A life of deep prayer and frequent reception of the sacraments— this is what "opens" us to the divine gift of love, like a bride opening to the gift of her bridegroom. Having received so great a gift, we are then able to share that love with others. This is the only context in which we can properly understand the authentically Christian vision of sexuality.

Chapter 8

THEOLOGY IN THE BEDROOM: A LIBERATING SEXUAL MORALITY

"Every man and every woman fully realizes himself or herself through the sincere gift of self. For spouses, the moment of conjugal union constitutes a very particular expression of this."
— John Paul II (LF 12)

In this brief introduction to John Paul II's Theology of the Body, we have examined our origin, our history, and our destiny, and the vocations of celibacy and marriage. Now we have the proper context in which to understand the Church's teaching on sexual morality.

Perhaps at this point you are feeling some trepidation. You have understood the Pope's logic, you can see where it is headed, and you know your life does not "measure up." Welcome to the human race. We all fall short of the glory (see Romans 3:23). But the good news is that Christ can restore us to glory. Remember—it does not matter where you have been or what mistakes you have made. The Theology of the Body is part of the message of salvation, not condemnation.

Authentic Christian morality is not against us. It is unstintingly *for* us. The first line in the *Catechism*'s section on morality speaks volumes. It is *not,* "Give up everything you really want and follow all these miserable rules or you're going to hell." It is "Christian, recognize your dignity" (CCC 1691). This is what John Paul II's Theology of the Body has been proclaiming all along—our dignity, our "greatness" as male and female. Now it is time to see it through. Be not afraid!

Applying the Basic Principle

At the close of the last chapter, I observed that all questions of sexual morality ultimately come down to one: Does this given act truly image God's *free, total, faithful, fruitful* love or does it not? My book *Good News About Sex and Marriage* uses this principle to answer 115 of the most common questions and objections to Church teaching. I refer you to that for a more detailed discussion. For now we'll just apply the principle to a few questions with the aim of arriving at the core of sexual morality.

If it challenges you, my challenge to you is to *let* it challenge you. We need not fear the demands of love. We need only fear that "hardness of heart" Christ spoke of that resists the demands of love (see Matthew 19:8). As you read the following questions, consider all we have learned about the "great mystery" of our creation as male and female and the call of the two to become "one flesh." Here we go.

Does masturbation image God's *free, total, faithful, fruitful* love or does it not? Does fornication (pre-marital sex) image God's *free, total, faithful, fruitful* love or does it not? Does adultery? Does homosexual behavior? Does lusting after pornographic images? And here is where the rubber hits the road (pun intended): Does an intentionally sterilized act of intercourse between spouses image God's *free, total, faithful, fruitful* love or does it not? If today you hear his voice, harden not your hearts (see Hebrews 3:15).

Wise men and women throughout history (including many non-Catholics) have recognized that respect for the procreative function of sexual union is the linchpin of all sexual morality. Even Sigmund Freud recognized this. He wrote that the "abandonment of the reproductive function is the common feature of all perversions. We actually describe a sexual activity as perverse if it has given up the aim of reproduction and pursues the attainment of pleasure as an aim independent of it" (*Introductory Lectures in Psychoanalysis*).

Consider this: When we divorce sex from its natural orientation toward new life, what is left to prevent the justification of any and every means to sexual climax? When we deliberately sterilize sex we fundamentally disorient the act. It no longer points of necessity to marriage and the raising of a family. Indulging libido for its own sake becomes the name of the game and we eventually treat natural, vaginal intercourse as only one of a-million-and-one ways of indulging libido. When we pry sex loose from its most natural consequence, we inevitably lose our moral compass. Welcome to the world in which we live.

Sex and Marriage Redefined

The monogamous, life-long union of the sexes and the family that results have served as the bedrock of Western civilization for centuries. Yet during the twentieth century, in only a few generations, sex, marriage, and the family have been radically deconstructed and redefined. Behaviors once commonly considered as an affront to human dignity and a serious threat to the social order are not only touted by the media as goods to be pursued, but are sanctioned and protected as legal "rights" by the government.

Have you ever wondered what brought about so radical a shift so quickly? The answer is complex, but one thing is certain: If the modern brand of sexual "liberation" was to flourish, the natural consequence of sex (procreation) *had* to be eliminated. The sexual revolution of the twentieth century is simply inexplicable apart from the nearly universal acceptance of contraception.

Proponents of contraception in the early 1900s knew that advancing their cause would be impossible without the "blessing" of the Christian churches. Until 1930, Catholics, Orthodox, and Protestants stood together in their condemnation of any attempt to deliberately sterilize the marital act. That year, the Anglican Church broke with more than 1,900 years of uninterrupted Christian teaching. When the Pill debuted in the early 1960s, the Catholic Church was the only Christian body retaining what in thirty short years had come to be seen as an archaic, even absurd position.

Inspired by a widespread but faulty view of the Second Vatican Council, many expected that a papal blessing of contraception was imminent. Withstanding unimaginable global pressure, Pope Paul VI shocked the world when he reaffirmed the traditional teaching against contraception in his 1968 encyclical letter *Humanae Vitae* (*Of Human Life*). It fell like a bomb. The widespread dissent that immediately followed has not ceased to this day.

We Need a "Total Vision of Man"

Was Paul VI hopelessly "out of touch" with reality? Or, maybe—just maybe—was he speaking a difficult, yet unchangeable truth to a world blinded by its excesses? If you have resisted the Church's teaching on contraception, believe me, I can relate. In fact, I almost left the Catholic Church because of this "blasted teaching." "Give me a break," I thought. "Denying people contraception is like denying people toothpaste or toilet paper. It is just another modern convenience. I should be able to express my love for my wife whenever I want without having to worry about raising fifteen kids!"

Pope Paul knew it would be difficult for the modern world to understand the immorality of contraception. Modern men and women have lost sight of the greatness, dignity, and divine purpose *of human life* (*Humanae Vitae*). When that happens, we no longer see the sexual union as a "great mystery" proclaiming God's love for humanity and foreshadowing heaven. We quickly reduce sex to a biological process subject to all sorts of human manipulations. Today, because of this mindset, most men and women give no more thought to tinkering with their fertility than they do to tinkering with their hair color.

Sex is certainly biological, but that is only a partial perspective. As Paul VI observed, in order to understand Christian teaching on sex and procreation, we must look "beyond partial perspectives" to a "total vision of man and of his vocation" (HV 7). This is what John Paul II set out to do in his Theology of the Body—provide the "total vision of man" that would enable us to understand the Church's teaching on contraception. In fact, John Paul II says that the entire TOB can be considered "*an extensive commentary on the doctrine contained precisely in Humanae Vitae*" (TOB 133:2).

All of our preceding reflections have led us to this point. If I have successfully introduced you to John Paul II's beautiful vision of the body and sex, the basic logic of *Humanae Vitae* should be fairly clear. But important questions raised by Paul VI's encyclical still remain. What particular insight does John Paul II's Theology of the Body offer us in understanding *Humanae Vitae*? Why does the Church reject contraception but accept natural methods of regulating fertility? What does the Church mean by the practice of "responsible parenthood"? Doesn't the Church's teaching against contraception impede couples from expressing their love for one another? Let's take a closer look. And remember: Be not afraid! The truth is not afraid of our questions. The question is, are we afraid of the truth? There is no need to be. It is the truth—and only the truth—that can set us free to love.

Ethics of the Sign

As the Pope writes, the teaching of *Humanae Vitae* "is strictly linked with our earlier reflections about *marriage in the dimension the (sacramental) sign*" (TOB 118:3). We can argue against contraception entirely from human reason and philosophy. But John Paul II shows the deepest *theological* reason for the immorality of contraception— it is fundamentally sacrilegious because it falsifies the sacramental sign of married love.

As a sacrament, marriage not only signifies God's life and love, it *really participates* in God's life and love—or, at least, it is meant to. For sacraments to convey grace (God's life and love), the sacramental sign must accurately signify the spiritual mystery. For example, as we mentioned in the last chapter, baptism, through the physical sign of immersion or infusion with water and the invocation of the Trinitarian formula, really and truly brings about a spiritual cleansing from sin. But if you were to baptize someone with mud or tar, no spiritual cleansing would take place because the physical sign is now one of making dirty. This would actually be a counter-sign.

All of married life is a sacrament. All of married life is meant to be a sign of God's life and love. But this sacrament has a consummate expression. Spouses signify God's love most profoundly than when they become "one flesh." Here, like no other moment in married life, spouses are called to participate in the "great mystery" of God's love. But this will only happen if their sexual union accurately signifies God's love. Therefore, as the Pope concludes, we can speak of moral good and evil in the sexual relationship based on whether the couple gives to their union "the character of a truthful sign" (TOB 37:6).

John Paul II says that the essential element for marriage as a sacrament is the language of the body spoken in truth. This is precisely how spouses "constitute" the sacramental sign of marriage (see TOB 104:9). By participating in God's eternal plan of love, the language of the body becomes "prophetic." As John Paul observes, the teaching of *Humanae Vitae* simply carries this truth to its logical conclusions (see TOB 123:2).

Insert contraception into the language of the body and (knowingly or unknowingly) the couple engages in a *counter-sign* of the "great mystery." Rather than proclaiming, "God is life-giving love," the language of contracepted intercourse says, "God is *not* life-giving love." In this way spouses (knowingly or unknowingly) become "false prophets." Contracepted sex denies and attacks our creation in the image of the Trinity at its roots. From this perspective we can see that contraception is a betrayal of the deepest truth of our humanity.

Fidelity to the Wedding Vows

Most couples who use contraception simply have no idea that this is what they are saying with their bodies, so this is not a matter of assigning culpability. But even if a couple is innocent in this regard, contraception will still have its damaging effect on their relationship. For example, if I drink a cup of poison, but do not know it is poison, I have not committed suicide and am not culpable for my own death. But it will still kill me. Whether I *think* it is poison or not has no bearing whatsoever on whether or not it *is* poison.

The causes of the dramatic rise in divorce in our culture are multiple and complex. Still, it should not surprise us in the least that the spike in divorce has coincided with the acceptance and practice of contraception. What is the connection? In short, as I asked in the last chapter, how healthy would a marriage be if a husband and wife were regularly unfaithful to their wedding vows? Sexual intercourse is meant to renew and express wedding vows. But contraception turns the "I do" of those vows into an "I do not."

During conjugal intercourse, a *"moment so rich in meaning,* it is ... particularly important that the 'language of the body' be re-read in truth" (TOB 118:4). We are free to choose whether to engage in sex. But if we choose to engage in sex, we are not free to change its meaning. The language of the body has "clear-cut meanings" all of which are "programmed," the Pope says, in the conjugal consent, in the vows. For example, to "the question: 'Are you ready to accept children lovingly from God ...?' the man and the woman answer, 'Yes'" (TOB 105:6, 106:3).

If spouses say "yes" at the altar, but then render their union sterile, they are lying with their bodies. They are being unfaithful to their wedding vows. Such dishonesty at the heart of the marital covenant cannot *not* have a deleterious effect.

Someone might retort, "Come on! I can commit to being 'open to children' at the altar, but this doesn't mean *each* and *every* act of intercourse needs to be open to children." But that makes as much sense as saying, "Come on! I can commit to fidelity at the altar, but this doesn't mean *each* and *every* act of intercourse needs to be with my spouse." If you can recognize the inconsistency of a commitment to fidelity ... *but not always*, you should be able to recognize the inconsistency of a commitment to being open to children ... *but not always*.

Perhaps another way out of this logic is simply for a couple to exclude "openness to children" in the commitment they make at the altar. Then a couple wouldn't be "lying" with their bodies by using contraception, would they? It would reflect what they committed to, yes. But what they committed to would not be to love as God loves. What they committed to would not be marriage. Indeed, as the Church has always recognized, willfully excluding openness to children renders a marriage null from the start.

Responsible Parenthood

So, does fidelity to the wedding vows imply that couples are to leave the number of children they have entirely to "chance"? No. In calling couples to a responsible love, the Church calls them also to a responsible parenthood.

Pope Paul VI stated clearly that those are considered "to exercise responsible parenthood who prudently and generously decide to have a large family, or who, for serious reasons and with due respect to the moral law, choose to have no more children for the time being or even for an indeterminate period" (HV 10). Notice that large families should result from prudent reflection, not "chance." Notice too that couples must have "serious reasons" to avoid pregnancy and must respect the moral law, the "ethics of the sign."

Assuming a couple has a serious reason to avoid a child (this could be financial, physical, psychological, etc.), what could they do that would not violate the consummate expression of their sacrament? In other words, what could they do to avoid conceiving a child that would not render them unfaithful to their wedding vows? You are doing it right now (I presume). They could *abstain* from sex. There is nothing wrong with abstaining from sex when there is a good reason to do so. The Church has always recognized that the *only* method of "birth control" that respects the language of divine love is "self-control."

A further question arises: Would a couple be doing anything to falsify their sexual union if they embraced during a time of natural infertility? Take, for example, a couple past childbearing years. They know their union will not result in a child. Are they violating "the sign" if they engage in intercourse with this knowledge? Are they contracepting? No. Contraception, by definition, is the choice to engage in an act of intercourse, but then do something else to *render* it sterile. This can be done by using various devices, hormones, surgical procedures, and the age-old method of withdrawal, or *coitus interruptus.*

Couples who use natural family planning (NFP) when they have a just reason to avoid pregnancy *never* render their sexual acts sterile; they never contracept. They track their fertility, abstain when they are fertile and, if they so desire, embrace when they are naturally infertile. Readers unfamiliar with modern NFP methods should note that they are ninety-eight to ninety-nine percent effective at avoiding pregnancy when used properly. Furthermore, any woman, regardless of the regularity of her cycles, can use NFP successfully. This is not your grandmother's "rhythm method."

What's the Difference?

To some people this seems like splitting hairs. "What's the big difference," they ask, "between rendering the union sterile yourself and just waiting until it is naturally infertile? The end result is the same: both couples avoid children." To which I respond, what's the big difference between killing Grandma and just waiting until she dies naturally? End result's the same thing: dead Grandma. Yes, but one is a serious sin and the other is not. It is exactly the same with contraception and NFP.

As John Paul II observes, the difference between periodic abstinence (NFP) and contraception "is much wider and deeper than is usually thought, one which involves in the final analysis two irreconcilable concepts of the human person and of human sexuality" (FC 32). The difference, in fact, is one of cosmic proportions.

First, it is important to realize that the Church has never said it is inherently wrong to avoid children. But the end (avoiding children) does not justify the means. There may well be a good reason for you to wish Grandma would pass on to the next life. Perhaps she is suffering terribly with age and disease. But this does not justify killing her. Similarly, you may have a good reason to avoid conceiving a child. Perhaps you are in serious financial straights. Perhaps you have four kids under the age of four and you have reached your emotional limits. But no scenario justifies rendering the sexual act sterile, just as no scenario justifies killing Grandma.

Grandma's natural death and a woman's natural period of infertility are both acts of God. But in killing Grandma or in rendering sex sterile, we take the powers of life *into our own hands*—just like the deceiver originally tempted us to do—and we make ourselves like God (see Genesis 3:5). Therefore, as the Pope concludes, "Contraception is to be judged so profoundly unlawful as never to be, for any reason, justified. To think or to say the contrary is equal to maintaining that in human life, situations may arise in which it is lawful not to recognize God as God" (Address, October 10, 1983).

Love or Lust?

One of the main objections to *Humanae Vitae* is that following its teaching (that is, practicing periodic abstinence when avoiding pregnancy) impedes couples from expressing their love for one another. But of what "love" are we speaking: authentic conjugal love that images God or its perennial counterfeit—lust?

God is the one who united marital love and procreation. Therefore, since God cannot contradict himself, a "true contradiction cannot exist between the divine laws pertaining to the transmission of life and those pertaining to the fostering of authentic conjugal love" (GS 51). It may well be difficult to follow the teaching of *Humanae Vitae*, but it could never be a contradiction of love.

Following this teaching is difficult because of the internal battle we all experience between love and lust. Lust impels us, and impels us very powerfully, towards sexual intercourse. But, as the future Pope observed in *Love and Responsibility*, if sexual intimacy results from nothing more than lust, it is not love. "On the contrary," he says, it "is a negation of ... love" (LR, pp. 150-151). In reality, what we often call love, "if subjected to searching critical examination turns out to be, contrary to all appearances, only a form of 'utilization' of the person" (LR, p. 167).

What purpose does contraception really serve? This might sound odd at first, but let it sink in. Contraception was not invented to prevent pregnancy. We already had a 100 percent safe, 100 percent reliable way of doing that—*abstinence*. In the final analysis, contraception serves one purpose: to spare us the difficulty we experience when confronted with the choice of abstinence. When all the smoke is cleared, contraception was invented because of our lack of self-control; contraception was invented to serve the indulgence of lust.

Why do we spay or neuter our dogs and cats? Because they cannot say no to their urge to merge; they are not free. If we deliberately deprive the conjugal act of its procreative purpose through contraception, we are reducing the "great mystery" of the one-flesh union to the level of animals. What distinguished us from the animals in the first place (remember original solitude)? *Freedom!* God gave us freedom as the capacity to love. Contraception negates this freedom. It says, "I can't abstain." Hence, contracepted intercourse not only attacks the procreative meaning of sex, "it also *ceases to be an act of love*" (TOB 123:6). If you cannot say no to sex, what does your "yes" mean? Only the person who is *free* with the freedom for which Christ set us free (see Gal 5:1) is capable of authentic love.

Chastity and the Integration of Love

Chastity, so often considered "negative" or "repressive," is supremely positive and liberating. It is the virtue that frees sexual desire from "the utilitarian attitude," from the tendency to *use* others for our own gratification. Chastity requires "an *apprenticeship in self-mastery* which is training in human freedom. The alternative is clear: either man governs his passions and finds peace, or he lets himself be dominated by them and becomes unhappy" (CCC 2339).

As we learned in chapter three, self-mastery does not merely mean resisting unruly desires by force of will. That is only the "negative" side of the picture. As we develop self-mastery, we experience it as "*the ability to orient* [sexual] reactions, both as to their content and as to their character" (TOB 129:5). The person who is truly chaste is able to direct erotic desire "toward what is true, good, and beautiful, so that what is 'erotic' also becomes true, good, and beautiful" (TOB 48:1). As spouses experience liberation from lust, they enter into the freedom of the gift which enables them to express the language of their bodies "in a depth, simplicity, and beauty hitherto altogether unknown" (TOB 117b:5).

It is certainly true that chastity requires "asceticism," understood as a ready and determined willingness to resist the impulses of lust. But, remember, authentic chastity does not repress. It enters into Christ's death and resurrection. As lust dies, authentic love is raised up. As the Pope expresses, "If conjugal chastity (and chastity in general) manifests itself at first as an ability to resist [lust], it subsequently reveals itself as a *singular ability* to perceive, love, and realize those meanings of the 'language of the body' that remain completely unknown to [lust] itself" (TOB 128:3). Hence, the discipline required by chastity does not impoverish or impede a couple's expressions of love and affection. Rather, "it makes them spiritually more intense and thus *enriches* them" (TOB 128:3).

Marital Spirituality

Such chastity, the Pope says, stands at the center of the spirituality of marriage (see TOB 131:2). What is "marital spirituality"? It is living according to God's in-spiration in married life. It involves spouses opening themselves to the indwelling power of the Holy Spirit and allowing him to guide them in all their choices and behaviors. The Pope says that sexual union itself—with all its emotional joys and physical pleasures—is meant to be an expression of "life according to the Holy Spirit" (see TOB 101:6). When spouses are open to the gift, the Holy Spirit infuses them "with everything that is noble and beautiful," with "the supreme value which is love" (TOB 46:5). But when spouses, because of their "hardness of heart," close themselves off to the Holy Spirit, sexual union quickly degenerates into an act of lust, an act of mutual exploitation.

Apart from the Holy Spirit, human weakness makes the teaching of *Humanae Vitae* a burden no one can bear. But to whom is this teaching given? To men and women enslaved by their weaknesses? Or to men and women set free by the *power* of the Holy Spirit? This is what is at stake in the teaching of *Humanae Vitae*—the power of the Gospel! The Church holds out the teaching of *Humanae Vitae* with absolute confidence in the fact that "God's love has been poured into our hearts through the Holy Spirit who has been given to us" (Romans 5:5).

Married couples "must implore [God] for such 'power' and for every other divine help in prayer ... they must draw grace and love from the ever-living fountain of the Eucharist; ...'with humble perseverance' they must overcome their own faults and sins in the sacrament of Penance. These are the means—*infallible and indispensable*—to form the Christian spirituality of conjugal ... life" (TOB 126:5). All of which, of course, presupposes faith, that openness of the human heart to the gift of the Holy Spirit.

If spouses are not living an authentic spirituality—in other words, if their hearts are closed to the transforming power of the Holy Spirit—they will inevitably view the

Church's teaching against contraception as an oppressive rule to follow. On the other hand, for couples who engage in their sexual embrace as an expression of "life according to the Holy Spirit," deliberately rendering their union sterile becomes unthinkable. They understand that their union is meant to signify Christ's life-giving love for the Church. In other words, they understand the theology of their bodies. Filled with "veneration for *the essential values of conjugal union*" (TOB 131:5), they are ready and willing to make every sacrifice necessary so that lust does not trump love.

I am far from being a perfect man and a perfect husband. I have a long way to go. But I also know, thanks to God's grace, that I have come a long way. This vision of marital spirituality is *real* to me. As I already said, at one point I almost left the Church because of her teaching against contraception. I saw it as an oppressive, arbitrary ethic. But when I finally let go of my stubborn pride and prayed, "OK, God, if this is true, you gotta change my heart," go figure, God started changing my heart. I continue gradually to experience the "ethos of redemption" in this area of my life. For those who live an authentic Christian ethos, the idea of engaging in contracepted intercourse becomes repulsive. Such people are free from the law! It doesn't feel imposed on them. It wells up from within as an expression of "life according to the Spirit." To the degree that such a change takes place in a person's heart, he begins to understand why the martyrs preferred to die rather than to break God's law. Again, I am not perfect, but I can attest to this ongoing transformation. And if this change is possible in my life, it is possible in anyone's life.

The Antithesis of Marital Spirituality

The Pope observes that life in the Holy Spirit leads couples to a profound awe and respect for the mystery of God revealed in their bodies. It leads couples to understand, among all the possible manifestations of love and affection, "the singular, and even exceptional meaning" of the sexual embrace (TOB 132:2).

Contraceptive practice—and the mentality behind it—demonstrates a total lack of understanding of the exceptional significance of the sexual embrace in God's plan. Such a lack, the Pope says, in a certain sense constitutes "the antithesis" of marital spirituality (see TOB 132:2). If marital spirituality involves spouses opening their bodies—and the "one body" they become in the sexual act—to the Holy Spirit, contraception marks a specific "closing off" to the Holy Spirit. Who is the Holy Spirit? As we say in the Nicene Creed every Sunday, he is "the Lord, the Giver of Life." Contraception says, "Lord and Giver of Life, we don't want you here."

Does not such a denial follow the pattern of original sin? In the act of creation, God had "in-spired" the human body with his own life and love (see Genesis 2:7). When man and woman sinned, they "ex-spired"; they breathed God's Spirit *out* of their bodies. Or, you might say, they refused the Spirit's penetration because of their "hardness of heart." So, once again, I appeal to you: If today you hear his voice, harden not your hearts! (Hebrews 3:15).

Sexual union, right from the beginning, was meant to participate in God's eternal exchange of love. Do you know what couples actually say with their bodies when they close their union to the Lord and Giver of Life? In short, whether they realize this or not, contracepted intercourse says, "We prefer the momentary pleasure of a sterlized orgasm over the opportunity of participating in the inner-life of the Trinity." To which I respond, *"Bad choice!"* But do you think if couples really knew they were choosing this, that they would continue to do so? I cannot help but think of Christ's words from the cross, "Father, forgive them; for they know not what they do" (Luke 23:34).

There is no tragedy in admitting we have sinned. There is no tragedy in admitting we have been duped by a counterfeit and sold a "pill" of goods. The only tragedy is the hardness of heart that refuses to admit its own sin. Be not afraid! As we have said so many times throughout this book, Christ came not to condemn but to save (see John 3:17). It does not matter how much lust has dominated your life. It doesn't matter how "dyslexic" or even "illiterate" you have been in reading the divine language of the body. As John Paul II boldly proclaims, through the gift of redemption "there is always the possibility of passing from 'error' to the 'truth'... the possibility of ... conversion from sin to chastity as an expression of a life according to the Spirit" (TOB 107:3).

Come, Holy Spirit, come! Convert our hearts from lust to love. Impregnate our sexual desires with divine passion so that, loving as God loves on earth, we might one day rejoice in the consummation of the "marriage of the Lamb" in heaven. Amen.

Chapter 9

SHARING THE THEOLOGY OF THE BODY IN A "NEW EVANGELIZATION"

At "the core of [the] Gospel ... is the affirmation of the inseparable connection between the person, his life and his bodiliness."
— John Paul II (EV 81)

If the future of humanity passes by way of marriage and the family (see FC 11), we could say that the future of marriage and the family passes by way of John Paul II's Theology of the Body. Put simply, there will be no renewal of the Church and of the world without a renewal of marriage and the family. And there will be no renewal of marriage and the family without a return to the full truth of God's plan for the body and sexuality. Yet this will not happen without a fresh theological proposal that compellingly demonstrates how the Christian sexual ethic—far from the cramped, prudish list of prohibitions it is assumed to be—is a liberating message of salvation that corresponds perfectly with the yearnings of the human heart.

This is precisely what John Paul II's Theology of the Body offers us. As such it provides the antidote to the culture of death and a theological foundation for the "new evangelization."

What is the New Evangelization?

John Paul used the expression "the new evangelization" during a trip to Latin America in 1983. Ever since he has "unstintingly recalled the pressing need for a *new evangelization*" (FR 103). This urgency stems not only from the fact that entire nations still have not received the Gospel, but also because "entire groups of the baptized have lost a living sense of the faith, or even no longer consider themselves members of the Church, and live a life far removed from Christ and his Gospel" (RM 86).

Therefore, one thing "new" about this evangelization is that it is directed in large part towards "baptized non-believers." Men and women in large numbers are "culturally Christian," but have not experienced a conversion of heart to Christ and his teachings. The call to interior conversion, in fact, was one of the main themes of Vatican II. As the Council understood well, this can only happen through an authentic, compelling, evangelical witness to salvation through Jesus Christ.

As John Paul clarified in his apostolic letter *At the Beginning of the New Millennium,* the new evangelization is not "a matter of inventing a 'new program.' The program already exists: it is the plan found in the Gospel and in the living Tradition, it is the same as ever" (NMI 29). What is essential in order to bring the Gospel to the modern world is a proclamation that is "new in ardor, methods, and expression" (Address, March 9, 1983).

Speaking to the American bishops in 1998, the Pope observed that "*the new evangelization* [involves] a vital effort to come to a deeper understanding of the mysteries of faith and to find meaningful language with which to convince our contemporaries that they are called to newness of life through God's love." It is the task of sharing with modern men and women "the 'unsearchable riches of Christ' and of making known 'the plan of the mystery hidden for ages in God who created all things' (Ephesians 3:8-9)" (SE 53, 55).

"How am I supposed to do that?" you ask. Here is a suggestion: talk about human sexuality in a prudent manner. What a great starting point for evangelization—everybody's interested! I say this with a bit of humor, but I am also entirely serious. If we are to make known to others "the plan of the mystery hidden for ages in God," as we have learned throughout this book, there is an image of this mystery stamped right in our sexuality. The Theology of the Body provides just the "meaningful language" we need "to convince our contemporaries that they are called to newness of life through God's love."

Bringing Heavenly Mysteries Down to Earth

Wouldn't you agree that the Pope's Theology of the Body—once it is presented in a way that people can understand—has a remarkable ability to bring the heavenly mysteries down to earth? The Pope's insights "ring true" because his teaching is the fruit of a constant confrontation of doctrine with experience.

As the Holy Father observes, "God comes to us in the things we know best and can verify most easily, the things of our everyday life, apart from which we cannot understand ourselves" (FR 12). What do we know better, what can we verify more easily, what is more "every day" than the experience of embodiment? This is where God meets us— *in the flesh.* And this is where we must meet the world in the new evangelization.

The *Catechism* teaches that the Church "in her whole being and in all her members ... is sent to announce, bear witness, make present, and spread the mystery of the communion of the Holy Trinity" (CCC 738). This sums up well the essential goal of evangelization. And this eternal mystery of *communion* becomes close to us, we realize that it is part of us through the lens of the Theology of the Body. The mystery of love and communion is not something "out there" somewhere. It is "right here"—stamped in our whole personal experience of "being a body," of being male or female.

Our creation as male and female and our longing for communion is "the fundamental fact" of human existence (see TOB 18:4). Again, the Gospel meets us right here. As John Paul says, the Christian mystery cannot be understood "unless we keep in mind the 'great mystery' involved in the creation of man as male and female and the vocation of both to conjugal love" (LF 19).

Incarnating the Gospel

In that same address to the American bishops quoted above, John Paul defined the basic task of evangelization as "the Church's effort to proclaim to [all men and women] that God loves them, that he has given himself for them in Christ Jesus, and that he invites them to an unending life of happiness" (SE 55). This basic message is in itself "good news." But it needs to be *incarnated* if men and women are to find their link with it.

Of course, this message was and *is* incarnated in Jesus Christ. But can't you just hear one of your friends or neighbors saying, "What does some man who lived two thousand years ago have to do with me?" As a professor of mine used to say, we can proclaim that "Jesus is the *answer*" til we are blue in the face. But unless people are first in touch with the *question*, we remain on the level of abstraction.

Herein lies the gift of grounding the Gospel in the body. It is the antidote to abstraction. It roots us in what is truly human—in the "every day"—and by so doing prepares us to receive what is truly divine. In other words, it puts us squarely in touch with the human question, thus opening our hearts to the divine answer.

In some sense, embodiment *is* the human question. What does it mean to be a man? What does it mean to be a woman? There are no more important questions for men and women to ask. And notice that these are inherently sexual questions, questions about "being a body."

Human Longing Leads to Christ

Of course, the very ability to question and to wonder flows from our deeper, spiritual dimension. But as we have learned throughout this book, the human anomaly is that our *spiritual* dimension is manifested in our *physical* dimension.

It was *in his body* that Adam realized he was "alone" in the world and that it was not good to be so. We are meant for love, for communion with an "other." This is what the body teaches us: we are destined for love. As John Paul II states so eloquently: "Man cannot live without love. He remains a being that is incomprehensible for himself, his life is senseless, if love is not revealed to him, if he does not encounter love, if he does experience it and make it his own, if he does not participate intimately in it. This ... is why Christ the Redeemer 'fully reveals man to himself'" (RH 10)—because his body "given up for us" reveals the truth about incarnate love.

The call to "incarnate love" is not abstract. Even if sin has distanced us from the beauty and purity of God's original plan, everyone knows the "ache" of solitude and the longing for communion. Everyone knows the "magnetic pull" of erotic desire. This basic human longing for union, in fact, is the most concrete link in every human heart with "that man who lived two thousand years ago." For all human longing, when purified, leads us to Christ, and none more so than the longing to unite with an "other" in the sexual embrace. "For this reason ... the two become one flesh." For what reason? To reveal, proclaim, and anticipate the union of Christ and the Church (see Ephesians 5:31-32).

The eternal, ecstatic, "spousal" Communion with Christ and the entire communion of saints—so far superior to anything proper to earthly life that we cannot begin to fathom it—this alone can satisfy the human "ache" of solitude. This is the North Pole to which that magnetic pull of erotic desire is oriented. Borrowing an idea from St. Augustine, we are made for communion with Christ, and our hearts are restless until we rest in this eternal embrace.

The Task of the New Evangelization

Sin's tactic is simply to "twist" and "disorient" our desire for heaven, our desire for Christ's eternal union with the Church. Recall our earlier observation that the sexual confusion so prevalent in our world and in our own hearts is nothing but the human desire for heaven gone berserk. The task of the new evangelization, then, is not to condemn the world for its excesses and distortions, but to help the world "untwist" them.

As the early Christian writer Tertullian said, the devil seeks to counter God's plan by plagiarizing the sacraments. That is all he can do—take what God created for our joy and happiness (the sacraments) and put his own branding on it. For example, the typical American college student quickly learns that the meaning of life is to get drunk and have rampant sex. "Untwist" these counterfeits and you discover two sacraments: the Eucharist and marriage.

We are meant to be "inebriated" on the new wine that Christ gives us. And where did Christ first reveal the gift of this new wine? At a wedding feast (see John 2). The union of the sexes can only bring us the joy we seek if it images Christ's love poured out in the Eucharist. This is what we really long for. In the new evangelization, we need to be able to walk into fraternity parties where people are getting drunk and seeking illicit sex and say, "Do you know what you really want here? You want the Eucharist and marriage, and the Catholic Church has them in their fullness."

Behind every sin, behind every disordered "acting out," there is a genuine human desire that is meant to be fulfilled through Christ and his Church. As our desires become "untwisted," we begin to realize that we really desire eternal love and joy. This is what we are created for. And the good news of the Gospel is that just such a love has been revealed. It is already been freely given. How? Where? In *the body* of Christ. *This* is why "Jesus is the answer."

If the spirit of the Gospel is not *incarnated* in this way with men and women's real desires, it will forever remain detached from what we experience as "essentially human." Yet Christ took on flesh to wed himself to what's essentially human. Hence, the Gospel of Jesus Christ is to be manifested with what is essentially human.

The Gospel of the Body

The "core of the Gospel," according to John Paul, "is the proclamation of a living God who is close to us, who calls us to profound communion with himself ... It is the affirmation of the inseparable connection between the person, his life and his bodiliness. It is the presentation of human life as a life of relationship." As a consequence, the Pope says that "the meaning of life is found in giving and receiving love, and in this light human sexuality and procreation reach their true and full significance" (EV 81).

We might call this profoundly incarnate vision the "gospel of the body." In a word, the Gospel is a call to communion. This is what we long for and this is what our bodies shout: *communion!* As John Paul asserts in his letter on the new millennium, "To make the Church *the home and school of communion*: that is the great challenge facing us in the millennium which is now beginning, if we wish to be faithful to God's plan and respond to the world's deepest yearnings" (NMI 43).

But we can only pass on this good news of love and communion—this "gospel of the body"—if we are first infused with it and vivified by it ourselves. As Pope Paul VI said in his great letter *On Evangelization in the Modern World*, "The Church is an evangelizer, but she begins by being evangelized herself" (EW 15). There is no doubt that, in delivering his Theology of the Body, John Paul II's intended audience was, first and foremost, the Church herself.

Very few Christians seem to understand that an image of the Gospel is stamped in their own bodies and in their yearning for union. Large numbers of Catholics have been caught up in the counterfeits of the day and are hostile towards the Church's teaching. Hence, unless the tide is turned within the Church—unless the Church is first evangelized—she cannot evangelize others.

The Spousal Analogy and the "Analogy of Faith"

John Paul II's Theology of the Body provides great hope for this urgently needed renewal within the Church. When we view the Gospel message through the interpretive key of man and woman's call to communion, not only does the Gospel message take on flesh, but even the most controversial teachings of the Church—contraception, divorce and remarriage, homosexuality, an all-male priesthood, etc.—begin to make beautiful sense.

Spousal theology demonstrates how all of the various puzzle pieces of the Christian mystery fit perfectly together. The truth of Catholicism "clicks" when viewed through the Theology of the Body. In other words, through the spousal analogy we become attentive to the "analogy of faith"—that is, to the coherence of the truths of faith among themselves and within the whole plan of Revelation centered on Christ (see CCC 90, 114, 158).

This is why the Theology of the Body will lead to a dramatic development of thinking about the tenets of our Creed. This is why the *Catechism* speaks of the important connection between sexual rectitude, believing in the articles of the Creed, and *understanding* the mysteries we profess in the Creed. In other words, the *Catechism* points to the intimate connection between purity of heart, love of the truth, and orthodoxy of faith (see CCC 2518).

Conversely, as the last few decades of dissent demonstrate, Christianity unravels at the seams—its inner logic collapses and so many of its core beliefs become contested—as soon as we divorce ourselves from the "great mystery" of spousal communion revealed through the body.

In Conclusion

Returning to an image we used previously, comparing John Paul II's grand vision of human sexuality to the impoverished vision we find in today's media is like comparing the luscious food at an elaborate banquet to the maggot-ridden scraps found at the bottom of a dumpster. And, yet, for lack of knowledge that such a banquet even exists—and that all without exception are invited to partake—our world continues to feed its hunger for love with such scraps. *Woe to us if we do not proclaim the gospel of the body from the rooftops! Woe to us if we do not invite everyone to the banquet!*

Only a microscopic percentage of people on this planet

have been exposed to the good news of the Theology of the Body. You are now one of them. What will you do with the scattered seeds that have fallen to you? I appeal to you, do not let the birds of the air eat them. Do not let the seeds die for lack of moisture. Do not let the cares of this world choke them off (see Luke 8:4-15). Tend to the soil and water the seeds by taking up a further, more in-depth study of the Pope's Theology of the Body (see the Resources section at the end of this book). Make it your mission in life to understand it, live it, and share it with everyone you know.

Understanding, living, and sharing the truth of your masculinity or femininity is not "yet another task" to add to your Christian life. Living according to the truth of our embodiment as male and female takes us to the heart of the Christian life. Remember that the Theology of the Body "concerns the whole Bible" (TOB 69:8) and plunges us into "the perspective of the whole Gospel, of the whole teaching, even more, of the whole mission of Christ" (TOB 49:3).

If the Theology of the Body provides the answer to the crisis of our times, it does so only because it reconnects the modern world with the "great mystery" of Christ and his Church. As John Paul II writes, "We are certainly not seduced by the naive expectation that, faced with the great challenges of our time, we shall find some magic formula. No, we shall not be saved by a formula, but by a Person, and the assurance which he gives us: *I am with you!*" (NMI 29). Christ the Bridegroom is with us! (see LF, part II)

This is our living hope. This is the hope that John Paul II offers us in his Theology of the Body. If we share this hope with the world, together, we shall not fall short of renewing the face of the earth.

Let it be, Lord, according to your will. Mary, woman of glory and star of the new evangelization, pray for us. Amen.

GLOSSARY

This glossary provides partial definitions of key terms and phrases for quick reference. Terms and phrases are listed in the order in which they appear in this book. In this way the glossary also serves as a summary of the book.

Chapter 1
WHAT IS THE THEOLOGY OF THE BODY?

1. *Theology of the body:* The study of how God reveals his mystery through the human body. This is also the title of John Paul II's 129 short talks on the subject.

2. *Incarnation:* The doctrine that refers to the Eternal Word, the second Person of the Holy Trinity, taking on human flesh and being born of a woman.

3. *Manichaeism:* An ancient dualistic heresy credited to Mani (or Manichaeus) that posits the source of evil in matter and therefore condemns the body and sex.

4. *Sacrament:* In its more ancient meaning, this refers to a physical sign that makes visible what is invisible. In its more strict meaning, sacrament refers to the seven signs of the new covenant (i.e., baptism, confirmation, Eucharist, penance, anointing of the sick, holy orders, and marriage) instituted by Christ to confer the grace of redemption.

5. *Spiritualized body:* Refers to the fact that the human body is "in breathed" not only with a spiritual soul but also, through the grace of redemption, with God's Holy Spirit.

6. *Divine mystery:* Refers to the two-fold "inner secret" of God: first, that God exists as a Trinity of persons in an

eternal "exchange of love" and, second, that God has destined man (male and female) to participate in this exchange of love.

7. *Communion of persons:* Refers to the unity or "common union" established when persons mutually give and receive "the sincere gift of self." The male-female communion of persons in marriage is a created image of *the* Communion of Persons found in the Trinity.

8. *Sincere self-giving:* Christ demonstrates that love is realized in and through self-donation. To say that man can only find himself through the "sincere gift of self" is to say that man can only realize who he is by loving as Christ loves.

9. *Spousal analogy:* Refers to the biblical use of marital love as an earthly image of God's love for Israel and, in the New Testament, Christ's love for the Church. Like all analogies, the spousal analogy is inadequate in communicating God's infinitely transcendent mystery. Yet, according to John Paul II, it is the most fitting human image of the divine mystery.

10. *Spiritual battle:* Refers to the conflict between good and evil that rages in us and all around us. The union of the sexes finds itself at the center of this great contest.

11. *Culture of death:* Refers to the utilitarian cultural milieu in which persons not only are treated as a means to an end, but—if they do not serve a given end—they are disregarded, mistreated, or even eliminated.

12. *Culture of life:* Refers to the cultural milieu in which human life is respected as the greatest of all gifts and every sacrifice is made to uphold each person's inestimable worth and value.

PART I: THE WORDS OF CHRIST

Chapter 2
BEFORE THE FIG LEAVES:
GOD'S ORIGINAL PLAN FOR THE BODY

13. *Original solitude:* Refers not only to Adam's experience of being "alone" without a helper, but also to the human experience of being "alone" in the visible world as a person made in God's image and likeness. Adam discovered his solitude by naming the animals and realizing he was fundamentally different from them.

14. *Freedom:* The capacity to *choose* and *determine* one's own actions. This is the main distinction between the human person and the animals.

15. *Person/subject:* These terms designate man's "greatness," the fact that he has an "inner life," an "inner self." Man is not merely some*thing* but some*one*. As a subject, a person can freely determine his own actions.

16. *Knowledge of good and evil:* Man has the capacity to distinguish between good and evil, but he is not free to determine what is good and what is evil.

17. *Original unity:* Refers to man and woman's experience of self-donating love and communion prior to sin. This unity resolved solitude in the sense of being without a "helper," but affirmed human solitude in the sense of being different from the animals. The original unity of man and woman in "one flesh" is worlds apart from the copulation of animals.

18. *Sacramentality of the body:* Refers to the body's capacity of making visible what is invisible. The body proclaims a "great mystery"—the spiritual mystery of God's Trinitarian love and our call to share in that love through Christ.

19. *Communion of persons* (see n. 7 above)

20. *Primordial sacrament:* Refers to marriage as the original and fundamental revelation of God's mystery in the created world.

21. *Original nakedness:* Refers to the original experience of nakedness without shame. Adam and Eve were untainted by shame because they had no experience whatsoever of lust. Before sin, man and woman experienced sexual desire as the desire to love in God's image.

22. *Shame:* In its negative sense, shame indicates that we have lost sight of the dignity and goodness of the body as a "theology"—a revelation of God's mystery. In its positive sense, shame indicates a desire to protect the goodness of the body from the degradation of lust.

23. *Lust:* Refers to sexual desire void of God's love. Lust leads a person toward *self-gratification* at the expense of the other, while love leads a person toward *self-donation* for the good of the other. Lust, therefore, is a *reduction* of the original fullness God intended for the sexual relationship.

24. *Interior gaze:* Refers to the "pure look" that Adam and Eve freely exchanged with one another in the state of innocence. It indicates not only a seeing of the body with the eyes; through that physical vision, they were able to gaze upon the interior truth of the person.

25. *Freedom of the gift:* This indicates that, prior to sin, man and woman did not experience sexual desire as a compulsion or uncontrollable urge. They were totally free and in this freedom they desired only to be a gift to each other. We are called in Christ to reclaim this freedom. It is for freedom that Christ has set us free (see Galatians 5:1).

26. *The original good of God's vision:* Taken from Genesis 1:31 ("God saw everything that he had made, and behold, it was very good."), this refers to the fact that everything God created is fundamentally good. Consequently, evil is not a reality in its own right, but is only and always a deprivation or reduction of the good that God created.

27. *Holiness:* Refers to the state of the person who loves rightly. God's holiness is manifested in his eternal exchange of self-giving love. Human holiness is what enables us to image God through the sincere gift of self. For the human person, as for the Incarnate Christ, holiness is manifested in and through the human body.

28. *Spousal love:* Refers to the love of "total self-donation." Marriage provides a model of such love, but it is not the only way of expressing the total gift of self.

29. *The spousal meaning of the body:* Refers to the call to love as God loves inscribed in the human body as male and female. If we live according to the spousal meaning of our bodies, we fulfill the very meaning of our being and existence (see n. 28 above).

30. *Universal call to holiness:* Refers to the fact that God calls everyone, without exception, to "love as he loves" through the sincere gift of self.

Chapter 3
THE ENTRANCE OF THE FIG LEAVES:
THE EFFECTS OF SIN AND THE REDEMPTION OF THE BODY

31. *Adultery committed in the heart:* This is committed when a person decides inwardly to treat another human being as an object to gratify lust rather than as a person to love in the image of God.

32. *The heritage of our hearts*: Refers to those deeper dispositions of our hearts that we have "inherited" not only through sin, but, more deeply, from the original experiences of man and woman. The heritage of our hearts goes deeper than lust and we still desire what is deeper; we still desire authentic love. Christ empowers us to live from that deeper heritage of our hearts.

33. *Questioning the gift*: Refers to the doubt that entered the human heart regarding God's disposition towards us. God's true disposition is one of self-donation ("gift"). With the dawn of sin we came to conceive of God, rather, as a tyrant who was withholding that which we desired.

34. *The second discovery of sex*: Refers to the experience after original sin in which the sexual relationship degenerated from one of love and communion to one of lust and domination.

35. *Lust* (see n. 23 above)

36. *Shame* (see n. 22 above)

37. *A living morality*: Refers to the "life" Christ offers us that enables and empowers us to desire and freely choose that which is true, good, and beautiful. It is to be distinguished from a sterile or "lifeless" approach to morality that, because of the allurement of evil, views God's law as a burden and an impediment.

38. *Ethic and ethos*: An ethic is an objective moral law or command. *Ethos,* on the other hand, refers to the abiding inner desires of the heart—what attracts and repulses a person. In the Sermon on the Mount, Christ demonstrates that the ethic is not enough ("You have heard the command ... but I tell you ..."). Christ came to transform our *ethos,* to change our hearts.

39. *The ethos of redemption* (also, *Christian ethos* or *new ethos*): This is characterized by a transformation of the human

heart such as to desire and to realize God's original plan for human life and the union of the sexes.

40. *Freedom from the law.* This is realized when, through the ethos of redemption, the heart is transformed to the point that it no longer needs "the law" (the ethic) because it does not desire to break it.

41. *Grace.* God's love poured into the human heart through the Holy Spirit. Grace enables men and women to "become who they are," to live and love as God intends. Grace penetrates the whole human person, body and soul, and enables us to "give up our bodies" through the sincere gift of self.

42. *Faith.* In its deepest essence, faith is the openness of the human heart to God's grace, to the divine gift, to the love poured into the human heart through the Holy Spirit.

43. *The grace of creation.* Refers to the gift of God's love poured out in the creation of the world and, in particular, the creation of man and woman. This grace enabled the first human couple to love one another in the divine image before the fall.

44. *The grace of redemption.* Refers to the gift of God's love poured out in the redemption of the world and, in particular, the redemption of man and woman. This grace enables men and women—to the degree that they take up their crosses and follow Christ—gradually to reclaim God's original plan and live it. The grace of redemption will come to total fulfillment in the resurrection of the body.

45. *Life according to the Spirit.* Refers to a life infused with the grace of redemption, that is, the life of the Holy Spirit. To the degree that we live "according to the Spirit" we are free from the law because our hearts conform to the law. Living according to the Spirit does

not mean we reject our bodies; it means we open our bodies to the Holy Spirit is inspiration.

46. *Life according to the flesh*: Refers to a life cut off from divine inspiration. Such a person is bound by lust and the other vices and so experiences God's law as a burden and imposition. This does not mean our flesh is "bad," but that our flesh needs to be inspired, that is, filled with God's Spirit.

47. *The redemption of the body*: To the degree that we experience "life according to the Spirit" we also experience the redemption of our bodies. This refers to the restoration of the human person in his or her integrity as a unity of body and soul. It affords the recovery of God's original plan in the human heart. This redemption is not only something we hope for in the resurrection from the dead. It is already at work in us within history.

48. *Purity of heart*: To the degree that we are pure of heart we understand, see, and experience the body as God created it to be, as a revelation of his own divine mystery. "Blessed are the pure in heart, for they shall see God" (Matthew 5:8).

49. *The interpretation of suspicion*: Those who live by this interpretation remain so locked in their own lusts that they project the same bondage onto everyone else. They cannot imagine any way to think about the human body and the sexual relationship other than through the prism of lust. This view is the antithesis of the meaning of life.

Chapter 4
BEYOND THE FIG LEAVES:
THE RESURRECTION OF THE BODY

50. *The resurrection of the body*: The doctrine that the human body is also destined for everlasting life in union with

the human soul. Eternal life is not only a "spiritual" reality. Man (male and female) is destined to share in the life of the Trinity as a body-person.

51. *The spiritualization of the body*: In the resurrection the body will be completely "spiritualized," which means not only the perfect integrity of body and soul, but also the perfect "indwelling" of the human body-person by the Holy Spirit (see also n. 5 above).

52. *The divinization of the body*: Since it is the divine Person of the Holy Spirit that will permeate the human body in the resurrection, the body will be in some way "divinized" or made divine. What God is by nature, we will participate in by grace. We will not lose our human nature, but through God's utterly gratuitous gift, men and women will participate—body and soul—in the divine nature (see 2 Peter 1:4).

53. *The Marriage of the Lamb*: The image used by the book of Revelation to describe the eternal union of Christ and the Church. Christ, the unblemished "Lamb of God," will forever make a gift of himself to his Bride, the Church, and the Church will return the gift of herself to Christ. Through this mutual exchange of love, God and man will live in eternal communion.

54. *The beatific vision*: The eternal vision of God granted to those who respond to the wedding invitation of the Lamb. The unsurpassed beauty and splendor of this eternal vision of God will fill all who behold with never-ending bliss.

55. *Fulfillment of the spousal meaning of the body*: In the resurrection, the spousal meaning of the body will be definitively revealed and fulfilled in receiving God's self-gift and returning the gift of self to God.

56. *Communion of saints*: Not only will the saints in heaven live in eternal communion with God, they will also live in eternal communion with each other. There

already exists a communion between those in heaven and those still journeying toward heaven on earth. In the resurrection, this communion of saints will fulfill definitively the unity of the human race which God willed from the beginning.

Chapter 5
CELIBACY FOR THE KINGDOM: A MARRIAGE MADE IN HEAVEN

57. *Eunuch for the kingdom of heaven*: Someone who chooses freely to forgo sexual intercourse in order to devote himself or herself totally to the "marriage of the Lamb."

58. *The "superiority" of celibacy*: This vocation is "better" not because of celibacy itself, but because the heavenly marriage (to which celibates devote themselves more directly) is objectively superior to the earthly marriage. Subjectively speaking, the "better" vocation is the one to which a given person is called.

59. *Manichaeism* (see n. 3 above)

60. *Complementarity of vocations*: Refers to the fact that Christian celibacy and Christian marriage do not conflict or compete with each other; rather, they enrich and complement each other. Marriage reveals the "spousal" character of celibacy just as celibacy reveals the sacramental orientation of marriage.

61. *Celibacy expresses the spousal meaning of the body*: Christian celibacy involves no rejection of the body and sexuality, but expresses the ultimate purpose and meaning of the body and sexuality by pointing so profoundly to the marriage of the Lamb. The celibate man or woman expresses the spousal meaning of the body by becoming a sincere gift to others. This leads, in turn, to a spiritual fruitfulness.

PART II: THE SACRAMENT

Chapter 6
MARRIAGE AS A DIVINE GIFT

62. *Mutual submission*: The apostle Paul makes use of the language of "submission" common in his day, but he exhorts spouses to a revolutionary understanding of it. Submission in Christian marriage is *mutual* and modeled not according to lust and domination, but according to the image of Christ and his Church.

63. *Reverence for Christ*: Spouses must submit to one another "out of reverence for Christ." This is nothing other than a spiritually mature form of the mutual attraction of the sexes. To the degree that we experience the redemption of sexual desire, the beauty of the opposite sex elicits not lust, but a deep awe and respect.

64. *Headship*: According to the "head and body" analogy employed by St. Paul, the husband is the head and the wife the body. The husband's headship calls him not to domination and authoritarian control, but to be the first to serve, to lay down his life for his bride (and children) in imitation of Christ.

65. *Sacramentality of the body* (see n. 18 above)

66. *Sacrament of creation*: Refers to the fact that God's "mystery of love" became most visible in creation through the "sign" of the union between man and woman.

67. *Sacrament of redemption*: Refers to the fact that God's "mystery of love" is definitively revealed in redemption through Christ's union with the Church, which St. Paul compares to the nuptial union of spouses.

Chapter 7
MARRIAGE AS A HUMAN SIGN OF GOD'S LOVE

68. *The language of the body:* Refers to the body's capacity to "speak" or "proclaim" God's love. It does so—or is meant to do so—most profoundly in the "one flesh" union of spouses. Here, spouses are meant to renew their marriage vows with their bodies.

69. *Agape:* The Greek word for divine love. Christ's love is *free, total, faithful,* and *fruitful.* In Christian marriage, *eros* and *agape* are called to meet and bear fruit. If spouses are to be faithful to the "language of their bodies," sexual intercourse must express *agape.*

70. *The prophetism of the body:* The body is "prophetic" because it is meant to proclaim God's love. However, we must be careful to distinguish between true and false prophets. If we can speak the truth with the body, we can also speak lies.

71. *"My sister, my bride":* This expression from the Song of Songs demonstrates that the lover recognizes that his beloved shares the same humanity he does. Calling her "sister" *before* calling her "bride" indicates that his motive is not one of lust, but of sincere self-giving.

72. *"A garden closed":* This expression from the Song of Songs indicates that the lover recognizes his beloved as "master of her own mystery." In other words, he sees and respects her dignity as an inviolable, self-determining person. The only way he can enter this "garden" is with her freely given "yes." If he were to manipulate her or barge through the door, he would violate her personhood.

73. *Test of life-or-death:* The marriage of Tobias and Sarah indicates that joining in "one flesh" takes spouses to the center of the great contest between good and evil, between life and death. But love is confident in the victory and is ready to do everything so that life conquers death.

Chapter 8
THEOLOGY IN THE BEDROOM:
A LIBERATING SEXUAL MORALITY

74. *Humanae Vitae:* Translated as *Of Human Life*, this is the title of Pope Paul VI's 1968 encyclical letter reaffirming the constant teaching of the Church on the immorality of contraception.

75. *A total vision of man:* Pope Paul VI stated in *Humanae Vitae* that in order to understand the Church's teaching on sexual morality, we need to view it in light of a total vision of man and of his vocation. Who is man? Why does he exist and what is he destined for? It is this "total vision of man" that John Paul II sketches in his Theology of the Body.

76. *Ethics of the sign:* The norm for sexual morality is whether or not a given behavior truly images or signifies the *free, total, faithful, fruitful* love of Christ. If it does not, it is a counterfeit for the love we truly desire.

77. *Responsible parenthood:* The integration of the faithful love of husband and wife in such a way that they participate fully, prudently, and generously in receiving children from God. Responsible parenthood does not deliberately frustrate the procreative potential of the conjugal act.

78. *Natural family planning:* Refers to those methods of family planning that are in keeping with God's plan for fertility and marital love. Modern methods of natural family planning are to be distinguished from the older and much less reliable "rhythm method." Modern methods of NFP are ninety to ninety-nine percent effective at avoiding pregnancy when used properly and can be used by any woman, regardless of the regularity or irregularity of her cycles.

79. *Chastity:* The virtue that orients sexual desire toward the supreme value of the person and the truth of self-giving love.

80. *Marital spirituality:* "Life according to the Spirit" (see n. 45 above) as applied to married life. It involves the openness of the spouses' bodies, and the "one body" they become, to the presence and indwelling of the Holy Spirit, the Lord and Giver of Life. Since contraception marks a "closing off" to the Lord and Giver of life, contraceptive practice and mentality are in some sense the "antithesis" of an authentic marital spirituality.

Chapter 9
SHARING THE THEOLOGY OF THE BODY
IN A "NEW EVANGELIZATION"

81. *New evangelization:* Refers to the urgent need to proclaim the "great mystery" of Christ's love to the whole world. What's "new" about this evangelization is not the message. Rather, it is the fact that this evangelistic effort is directed largely towards "baptized non-believers." If the Church is to reach modern men and women with the Gospel, her proclamation must be "new in ardor, methods, and expression."

82. *Incarnating the Gospel:* This means demonstrating that God's plan of love for humanity is not "out there" somewhere. It is "right here" in our everyday experience of being male and female and in our longing for communion. If the Gospel is not *incarnated* in this way, it will forever remain detached from what is "essentially human."

83. *Incarnate love:* Love is supremely spiritual. The human paradox, however, is that the spiritual is manifested in the body. It is in *our bodies* that we experience the divine call to love and self-donation. This is why Christ "fully reveals man to himself"—because he reveals the truth about incarnate love by "giving up his body" for us.

84. *Gospel of the body:* If the Gospel is the "good news" of our salvation in Christ, the expression "gospel of the

body" indicates that the human body is a sign and instrument of the same message of our salvation in Christ. In a word, the Gospel is a call to communion. This is what our bodies shout as male and female: *communion!*—"and I mean in reference to Christ and the church" (Ephesians 5:32).

85. *Analogy of faith*: Refers to the coherence of the truths of faith among themselves and within the whole plan of God's Revelation. There is an inter-connectedness of the truths of faith, each one being integrally related to the others. The Theology of the Body helps demonstrate how the various puzzle pieces of the Christian mystery fit beautifully together.

Resources

The following is a partial list of resources and organizations that can assist you in your further study of John Paul II's Theology of the Body.

Other Resources by Christopher West

Books

- *Good News About Sex and Marriage: Answers to Your Honest Questions about Catholic Teaching* (Servant, 2000)

- *Theology of the Body Explained: A Commentary on John Paul II's "Man and Woman He Created Them"* (Pauline, 2003; revised edition, 2007)

- *The Love That Satisfies: Reflections on Eros and Agape* (Ascension Press, 2007)

- *Heaven's Song: Sexual Love as It Was Meant to Be* (Ascension Press, 2008)

Audio & Video Presentations

- Christopher West has an extensive collection of audio and video presentations available for personal or group study. Visit AscensionPress.com or ChristopherWest.com or call 1-800-376-0520 for more information.

Official Web Site

- Visit ChristopherWest.com or TheologyoftheBody.com for information on Christopher's speaking schedule, downloadable articles and sound files, or to purchase his books and other resources.

Books, CDs, and Other Resources

Ascension Press

- Ascension Press is Christopher West's official media company. They also distribute the audio and video products of other well-known Catholic speakers.
- Visit AscensionPress.com or call 1-800-376-0520.

GIFT Foundation

- This non-profit, lay apostolate offers a variety of audio and video resources on the Theology of the Body, Natural Family Planning (NFP), and related topics.
- Visit giftfoundation.org or call (847) 844-1167.

Our Father's Will Communications

- Offers audio and video products by speakers like Fr. Thomas Loya, Katrina Zeno, David Sloan, Christopher West, and many more.
- Visit theologyofthebody.net or call 1-866-333-OFWC.

Pauline Books and Media

- Publishers of John Paul II's *Man and Woman He Created Them: A Theology of the Body* (2006) and Christopher West's *Theology of the Body Explained: A Commentary on John Paul II's "Man and Woman He Created Them"* (2007).
- Visit pauline.org or call 1-800-876-4463.

Real Love Productions

- Books, videos, and other resources by Mary Beth Bonacci. In her dynamic presentations, Mary Beth draws from the Theology of the Body to support teens, young adults, and parents in their quest for a true understanding of what it means to love and be loved.
- Visit reallove.net or call 1-888-667-4992.

Organizations

The Alexander House

- The Alexander House is a non-profit, lay apostolate dedicated to marriage education and enrichment through the teachings of the Catholic Church, especially John Paul II's Theology of the Body. They assist married couples, troubled couples, engaged couples, young adults, high school/middle school youth, priests, and dioceses. They are particularly skilled at helping couples integrate the principles of the Theology of the Body into their relationship through their "marriage coaching" program.
- Visit thealexanderhouse.org

Family Honor

- Family Honor provides resources and programs based on the Theology of the Body to help parents and children grow together in their understanding of God's plan for life and human sexuality.
- Visit familyhonor.org or call 1-877-208-1353

Theology of the Body Evangelization Team (TOBET)

- Engages in activities of evangelization, apologetics, education, charity, and mission through the use of various media with a focus on Pope John Paul II's Theology of the Body.
- Visit tobet.org

Theology of the Body Institute

- The Theology of the Body Institute is a non-profit educational organization promoting the Theology of the Body at the popular level of both the Christian and the secular cultures. It works with key bishops to develop a certification program for catechists. Through graduate level courses (offered in a five-day intensive format throughout the year), on-site lecture programs, and clergy

training, the Theology of the Body Institute seeks to educate and train men and women to understand, live, and promote the Theology of the Body.
- Visit TOBInstitute.org

Theology of the Body International Alliance (TOBIA)

- This is a support network providing resources for those striving to evangelize the world by means of Pope John Paul II's understanding of the human person, explained in his works *Love and Responsibility* and *Theology of the Body*. Great resource for help in starting a study group.
- Visit theologyofthebody.net and click on "TOBIA"

Love and Responsibility Foundation

- This organization is dedicated to promoting the teachings of Pope John Paul II on marriage and the family.
- Visit catholicculture.com

Women Affirming Life

- Offers "A New Language" study series on the Theology of the Body by Professor Mary Shivanandan of the John Paul II Institute. This is a four-season group study series, each consisting of six weekly sessions.
- Visit affirmlife.com or call (617) 254-2277.

Women of the Third Millennium (WTTM)

- This is a lay organization co-founded by Katrina Zeno and Zoe Romanowsky in response to John Paul II's call for women to develop a "new feminism." WTTM offers a variety of retreats for women and men.
- Visit wttm.org or call (740) 282-9062.

Graduate School

John Paul II Institute for Studies on Marriage & Family

- This pontifical institute is a graduate school of theology founded by Pope John Paul II to help the Church understand more fully the human person, marriage, and family in light of divine revelation. Campuses of the Institute exist in many countries throughout the world.
- Visit johnpaulii.edu for the American campus and jp2institute.org for the Australian campus.

ACKNOWLEDGMENTS

My thanks to the following men and women who helped with this book:

- All of those at Pauline Books and Media who invested in my book *Theology of the Body Explained,* upon which this short introduction is based.

- Michael Waldstein for the superb research and careful scholarship that went in to the new translation of John Paul II's catechesis.

- Greg Weidman, Nathan West, Matthew Pinto, Dana Vink, and Daniel Weiss for reviewing the manuscript and offering many helpful suggestions.

- The entire team at Ascension Press for all their work in bringing this book to print.

- Annamarie Adkins, Tracy Moran, Michael Flickinger, Michael Fontecchio, Michael J. Miller, and Steven Motyl for their editorial and technical assistance.

- Barry Pine for pushing me when I needed it.

- My wife, Wendy, for her unfailing love and support.

ABOUT THE AUTHOR

Christopher West—renowned educator, best-selling author, and popular theologian—serves officially as a research fellow and faculty member of the Theology of the Body Institute in suburban Philadelphia. His week-long courses offered through the Institute draw students from around the world.

As one of the most sought-after speakers in the Church today, Christopher has lectured on four continents, in more than a dozen countries, and in well over 200 American cities. He has been seen defending the faith on Fox News, MSNBC, and ABC News, and has been heard on numerous national radio shows. His multiple books, study guides, and CD and DVD presentations reach an international audience.

Of all his titles, Christopher is most proud to call himself a devoted husband and father. He lives near Lancaster, Pennsylvania, with his wife, Wendy, and their five children.